ALL ABOUT
GRILLING

Joy
of
Cooking

ALL ABOUT
GRILLING

IRMA S. ROMBAUER
MARION ROMBAUER BECKER
ETHAN BECKER

PHOTOGRAPHY BY TUCKER & HOSSLER

SCRIBNER
NEW YORK • LONDON • TORONTO • SYDNEY • SINGAPORE

SCRIBNER
1230 Avenue of the Americas
New York, NY 10020

WELDON OWEN INC.
Chief Executive Officer: John Owen
President: Terry Newell
Chief Operating Officer: Larry Partington
Vice President, International Sales: Stuart Laurence
Publisher: Roger Shaw
Creative Director: Gaye Allen
Associate Publisher: Val Cipollone
Associate Editor: Anna Mantzaris
Consulting Editors: Norman Kolpas, Judith Dunham
Designers: Jamie Leighton, Sarah Gifford
Photo Editor: Lisa Lee
Production Director: Stephanie Sherman
Production Manager: Chris Hemesath
Production Assistant: Donita Boles
Studio Manager: Brynn Breuner
Food Stylists: Kim Konecny, Erin Quon
Step-by-Step Photographer: Mike Falconer
Step-by-Step Food Stylist: Andrea Lucich

Joy of Cooking All About series was designed
and produced by Weldon Owen Inc.,
814 Montgomery Street, San Francisco,
California 94133

Set in Joanna MT and Gill Sans

Separations by Bright Arts Singapore.
Printed in Singapore by Tien Wah Press (Pte.) Ltd.

10 9 8 7 6 5 4 3 2 1

Library of Congress Cataloging-in-Publication Data
is available.

ISBN 0-7432-0643-6

Recipe shown on half-title page: *Grilled Pork Chops*, 69
Recipe shown on title page: *Grilled Lamb Chops*, 73

CONTENTS

FOREWORD

Outdoor cooking enthusiasts "do best when they stick to simple methods," wrote my mom in the 1962 edition of the Joy of Cooking. "We never attend a patio barbecue featuring paper chef's hats, aprons with printed wise-cracks, striped asbestos gloves, an infra-red broiler on white-walled wheels and yards and yards of extension cord and culinary red tape," she continued, tongue emphatically in her cheek, "without anticipating a deservedly heavy thunderstorm."

The simple aim of this volume in the new All About series is to cut the culinary red tape so often associated with grilling. It explains the most efficient and effective ways to cook outdoors, while offering a wide selection of easy-to-follow, backyard-tested recipes for the many different kinds of food we all love to cook in the open air.

You might notice that this collection of recipes is adapted from the latest edition of the Joy of Cooking. Just as our family has done for generations, we have worked to make this version of Joy a little bit better than the last. As a result, you'll find that some notes, recipes, and techniques have been changed to improve their clarity and usefulness. Since 1931, the Joy of Cooking has constantly evolved. And now, the All About series has taken Joy to a whole new stage, as you will see from the beautiful color photographs of finished dishes and clearly illustrated instructions for preparing and serving them. Granny Rom and Mom would have been delighted.

I'm sure you'll find All About Grilling to be both a useful and an enduring companion in your kitchen.

Enjoy!

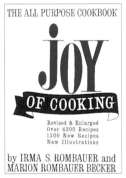

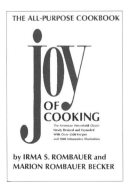

Ethan Becker pictured with his grandmother, Irma von Starkloff Rombauer (left), and his mother, Marion Rombauer Becker (right). Irma Rombauer published the first Joy of Cooking *at her own expense in 1931. Marion Rombauer Becker became coauthor in 1951.* Joy *as it has progressed through the decades (from top left to bottom right): the 1931 edition with Marion's depiction of St. Martha of Bethany, said to be the patron saint of cooking, "slaying the dragon of kitchen drudgery"; the 1943 edition; the 1951 edition; the 1962 edition; the 1975 edition; and the 1997 edition.*

About Grilling

Grilling is cooking food directly over live heat (either charcoal or gas), almost always uncovered and usually at fairly high temperatures. Barbecuing is a traditional, covered, slow-cooking method, usually for larger cuts of highly seasoned meats, employing relatively low, indirect heat from charcoal or wood. Grill-roasting involves large cuts of meat, poultry, or whole fish cooked in a covered grill using indirect heat (the food is not directly over the coals).

The central fact about grilling is that it is generally a high-heat cooking method, which involves cooking relatively tender foods quickly over a hot fire. When food is exposed to the direct heat of the flames, a seared crust develops on its exterior. Tender cuts of meat, such as beef, pork, or lamb, grill beautifully, as do shrimp, scallops, and firm-textured fish, such as tuna, swordfish, and mahimahi.

Steaks and chops are extraordinarily well suited to grilling. Avoid excessively thick cuts, which tend to char outside before they are cooked through; an inch and a half should be the thickness limit for individual servings. Oil the cooking grate before you begin grilling.

Grill Options

Most outdoor grills fall into one of two categories: open and covered. Open grills range in size and portability from the simple, small hibachi **(1)** to large built-in units. An open grill is most useful if it has a heavy grate (to transfer heat and give beautiful grill marks) and an adjustable firebox or grate (to help control the intensity of heat).

Covered grills come in many styles, but the covered kettle grill **(2)** ranks high. Neither the charcoal grate on which the coals rest nor the cooking grate is adjustable, and the most popular units were designed to be used with the lid, to reduce the possibility of flare-ups and to speed cooking by circulating heat around the food.

Gas grills **(3)** have come a long way in the past few years, most notably in burning fuel more efficiently and in their ability to achieve the higher temperatures crucial for a delectable brown crust.

Unfortunately, the so-called stove-top grills—basically some variety of metal grid that fits over a stove burner, equipped with a pan to catch dripping grease—do not get hot enough to really grill. If you want to grill inside and you have a fireplace, consider the Tuscan grill. Although difficult to find, this handy device consists of a simple metal frame that holds an adjustable grilling grate, suitable for use in indoor fireplaces. To rig one of your own, remove the grill rack from any standard outdoor grill and use bricks to support it in the fireplace.

Fuel for the Fire

Grilling has become synonymous with little pillow-shaped charcoal briquettes, available in every supermarket. Because they are not pure charcoal but rather a combination of charcoal, sawdust, powdered scrap lumber, starch, and additives, briquettes can impart unpleasant flavors. Hardwood lump charcoal, made by burning hardwood in a closed container, is worth searching out in hardware and specialty stores.

These chunks of almost pure carbon light more easily, give heat that is more responsive to changes in oxygen, and burn cleaner and hotter than briquettes. A wide variety of wood chips on the market—ranging from mesquite to cherry to hickory—can be added to glowing charcoal to give a smokier flavor. But unless the food spends more than a few minutes on the grill, the smoke will have little time to penetrate.

Necessary Tools

One of the joys of grilling is the fact that it is a simple cooking method. So why clutter it up with unnecesary gadgets? In the final analysis, you really need a few basics—just a fire, a grid, and some food to cook. However, a handful of tools are very helpful. They can make the difference between enjoying your day or igniting your temper.

Heavy-duty, long-handled, spring-loaded tongs: These are indispensable to the griller. Use them to put food on the grill, move it around quickly and easily, and take it off, all without dropping anything or burning your arms. Make sure the tongs are heavy duty so they will not bend when you lift heavy pieces; have long handles so you can work over a hot fire safely; and are spring-loaded so they are always ready for use.

Offset spatula: This is handy for moving items that are not easily moved with tongs, such as burgers or fish fillets. The bent neck keeps your hand farther from the heat and provides leverage.

Long-handled fork: This is not for moving items around on the grill—you do not want to unnecessarily pierce food and let juices escape. The fork is useful, though, for picking up the grid when you need to add more coals, for stirring the coals around, and for piercing food to test for doneness.

Stiff wire brush: This tool is essential for cleaning the grill surface. It is easiest to do this immediately after cooking, before any grease has congealed and while the hot coals will disintegrate any food residue that falls into them.

Aluminum foil pans: Available at any supermarket, these containers are useful for transporting raw ingredients from kitchen to grill and cooked ingredients from grill to table.

Skewers: These come in all varieties, from inexpensive bamboo models to stainless-steel numbers with ornate brass finials.

Dish towels: Folded over, dish towels are perfect for handling hot dishes or skewers and for wiping up all sorts of spills.

Starting the Fire

Starter fluid or presoaked charcoal briquettes should be avoided. Because fumes are released throughout the cooking process, the taste of the food can be affected.

To start a fire in the simplest fashion, crumple several sheets of newspaper in the bottom of the grill beneath the fire grate, set the grate back in place over the newspapers, and lay several handfuls of twigs or kindling on the grate. Next, top the twigs with a rather loose tepee-shaped arrangement of slightly larger twigs (or several handfuls of charcoal, if that is your fuel of choice) and light the newspaper. When the wood or charcoal is well lit—about 5 minutes for wood, 15 minutes for charcoal—add additional fuel.

If the fuel is charcoal, you can start your fire with an electrical coil starter instead of paper and twigs. These electrical coils, attached to a power cord by means of a plastic handle, are reliable and consistent. To use a coil fire starter, remove the cooking grill and place the starter right on the fire grate. Mound charcoal on top of the starter and plug it into a grounded outlet. As the element becomes red hot, it will ignite the charcoal that is in contact with it. At this point, you can unplug the starter and remove it; the hot coals will ignite the others. To prolong the life of your electric starter, don't let it cool down in the fire; instead, remove it as soon as the coals are lit, unplug it, and set it aside on a fire-proof surface, out of reach of children, until it is cool.

The chimney starter, also known as a flue starter, is a paragon of efficiency, reliability, and economy. It is basically a sheet-metal cylinder, open at both ends, with a grid set inside the flue several inches from the bottom. Fill the bottom section with crumpled newspaper, then fill the top with charcoal and light the newspaper. When the charcoal is red hot, dump it out and put as much additional charcoal as you want on top of it.

If you find yourself ready to grill and realize you don't have a chimney starter, you can make a perfectly acceptable substitute by removing both ends from a large coffee can and punching a few ventilation holes along the bottom edge with a can opener.

Whatever lighting method you use, light the fire far enough in advance to ensure an even, flameless fire of the proper temperature (15 to 40 minutes, depending on your fuel). Allow enough time for the fuel to get fiery red and then die down until it is just covered with gray ash. This is the point at which you are ready to cook.

GRILLING PRECAUTIONS

We advise taking a few cautionary measures when grilling:

- For safety's sake always set your grill on level ground in the largest possible open space, away from walls, wooden fences, overhanging eaves or tree branches, or anything else that might easily catch fire.
- Keep toddlers well away from the grill, and do not let older children run or play too close to the grilling area. Keep pets away, too.
- If using charcoal-fired equipment, do so with adequate ventilation, where the carbon monoxide fumes can be carried off completely.
- Do not ever use charcoal grills in a house, tent, cabin, garage, or other enclosed area. Insufficient ventilation may prove fatal.
- Never light the fire with gasoline, and never spray lighter fluid onto lit coals. Do not use excessive lighter fluid; always follow manufacturer's directions.
- It is always a good idea to have handy a fire extinguisher or a bucket of sand for extinguishing uncontrollable flare-ups.
- Fire goes out without oxygen; so fires in covered grills can be extinguished by closing the lid and vents.

HOW TO START A FIRE

There are at least three good alternatives to starting a fire with starter fluid and presoaked charcoal briquettes. Here we use a covered kettle grill to illustrate all three methods.

1 For the first method, start by crumpling several sheets of newspaper and putting them in the bottom of the grill. Set the fire grate over the newspapers.

2 Lay several handfuls of twigs or kindling on the fire grate.

3 Top the twigs with a loose tepee-shaped arrangement of slightly larger twigs or several handfuls of charcoal and light the newspaper. Light the newspapers and let the fire burn until well lit. Add more fuel to the fire as needed.

4 The second method of starting a fire employs an electric coil. Place the electric coil right on the fire grate. Mound charcoal on top of the coil and plug it into a grounded outlet. When the element ignites the charcoal immediately around it, unplug it and set it in a safe place to cool. Add more fuel to the fire as needed.

5 The third method employs a chimney starter. Set the chimney on the fire grate. Fill the bottom section with crumpled newspaper, then fill the top with charcoal and light the newspaper. When the charcoal is red hot, dump it out. Add more fuel to the fire as needed.

6 Once the fire is lit and the coals are fiery red in the center and covered with ash, put the grill rack in place and begin grilling.

Getting to the Grill

With your grill and fuel chosen, your fire started and at the proper temperature, and your tools at hand, you are ready to actually put food over flame.

Although grilling is a very versatile cooking method, not every food is suitable for the grilling fire. Because grilling involves cooking quickly over high heat, it is most suitable for foods that will cook to the desired degree of doneness on the interior before being incinerated on the exterior. Tender cuts of meat with little connective tissue, like steaks, chops, or pork loin, are excellent choices, as are firm-textured fish like tuna, swordfish, or mahimahi. In the shellfish category, shrimp, scallops, and lobster are wonderful. Just avoid trying to grill foods that are either too mushy (tofu or delicate fish, such as cod, flounder, or sole) or too stringy (meats like beef brisket).

Whatever food you are cooking, it is important not to crowd the grill surface. If the edges of your tomatoes or steak or pork chops are touching, they will not cook properly. More important, if the grill is crowded with food, you will have lost the key ability to move food around to hotter and cooler spots to regulate its cooking.

Since every live fire is unique, grilling is an inexact science. This means the griller must be able to judge the fire temperature. There is an easy and effective way, however, to shorten the hundreds of grilling hours that it takes to tell from a glance or a poke just when a particular steak or fillet of fish is perfectly cooked: cut a portion open and look inside. There is no better method of knowing when your food is cooked the way you like it—it will not hurt the food, and it sure beats serving raw chicken or shoe-leather pork. If you feel that the cutting mars the perfect appearance of the food, keep the tested portion for yourself.

Spit-Roasting and Rotisserie Cooking

Spit-roasting and rotisserie cooking (the terms are interchangeable) are best for small or large fowl, whole joints like leg of lamb, and other chunky cuts of meat. Some grills include a spit, which is usually protected from wind by a metal shield on three sides. Consult the directions that come with a spit to determine the maximum weight it will support—probably ten pounds for roast meat and up to fifteen for fowl. Smaller birds should be strung traversely on the spit, larger ones head to tail along the spit's axis.

Remember that because of the high heat of spit-roasting, the weight losses due to shrinkage can be great and flare-ups from dripping fat frequent. (In olden days, spit-roasting was done in front of a fire, not over it, thus avoiding too strong a heat and any flare-ups.) Flare-ups can be avoided in part by careful trimming of surplus fat. Some short flare-ups may be desired for browning; unwanted ones can be doused with a spritz of water from a spray bottle.

JUDGING THE FIRE'S TEMPERATURE

Not all foods should be cooked over the same temperature fire. While red meats generally do best over a very hot fire, fish and vegetables often prefer a less hot fire, and tender fare such as fruits do best over a cooler fire.

This means the griller must be able to judge the temperature of his or her fire. The method used to do this is simple: you see how hot the fire makes your skin. To judge the temperature, wait until the coals are covered with ash. Hold your hand about five inches above the cooking surface. If you can hold it there for five to six seconds, you have a low fire; three to four seconds, medium; and one to two seconds, hot.

Grill-Roasting or Indirect Grilling

In this hybrid method, whole chickens, turkeys, legs of lamb, and the like are roasted by the indirect heat of the fire in a covered grill, as if in a smoky oven. To grill-roast, build a fire in your grill in the usual manner and push all the coals to one side or around the perimeter. (For a gas grill, heat the entire fire bed; then before cooking, turn off the gas jets under the back of the grill on which the food will go.) On the other side, or in the center, place a drip pan if you wish to collect juices or fill the cooking kettle with the steam from aromatic liquids.

When you put the food on the cooking grate, place it over the area that has no coals and over the drip pan if you are using one. Then set the grill cover in place, making sure no portion of the item you are cooking is directly over the fire. Adjust the vents as necessary, or adjust the gas burner control, to maintain the temperature between 250° and 300°F; an oven thermometer, set close to the food, will help you determine the temperature of the environment. Use an instant-read thermometer to test food for doneness.

Cooking in Ashes

Ash cooking is best done in a fireplace or campfire. The food you are preparing should be cut into relatively small pieces so that it will cook through before browning too much at the edges. And it is a good idea to keep the batches of food small, so the packets are not too unwieldy to take in and out of the coals. Although hamburger with potatoes and onions may be classic, bone-in chicken, root vegetables, sausages, and meaty fish—seasoned with herbs, garlic, and olive oil—are also wonderful candidates for ash cooking. You can also bake apples in this way, coring them and then stuffing them with chopped nuts, sugar, and butter before wrapping them in aluminum foil.

Wrapping the food properly requires three sheets of heavy-duty aluminum foil, each about 2 feet long. Start by spreading the food over the center of the first sheet, then lay the second length on top. Fold the edges of the two sheets together on all sides, closing the pack, then roll them up until they bump into the food, forming a ridge around its perimeter. Place the pack folded side up in the center of the third sheet of foil and fold the four sides over the top of the packet, one after the other.

Whether wood or charcoal is the fuel, the fire should have passed its peak of intensity and be dying down—nothing but glowing coals covered with gray ash. Sweep the coals to the side, leaving your "cooking surface" covered with hot ashes. Lay in the packets and surround with the coals. The only way to check for doneness is to open a packet and take a peek.

ABOUT GRILLING **SEAFOOD**

Grilling is an ideal technique for cooking many fish. The intense heat complements the flavor of the fish by charring its surface; often, little more added flavor is needed, so you can keep seasonings to a minimum.

Certain fish—especially the most delicate whitefish and thin fillets—are virtually impossible to grill; they simply fall apart when you try to turn them over. Some whole fish are also tricky. Best for grilling are thick steaks of swordfish, salmon, tuna, and the like; small, firm whole fish such as mackerel, pompano, and red snapper; and, of course, many varieties of shellfish.

Generally, shellfish do not stick to the grill, or do so only minimally, so they are much easier to grill than finfish. And you have more latitude in timing when grilling shellfish, because they are much more forgiving. If you overcook most finfish, they will fall apart on the grill. Overcook shellfish, however, and they will simply dry out; you will lose some of their pleasures, but at least you will still be able to serve them.

Teriyaki Grilled Salmon Steaks, 20

Grilling Fish

Generally, you want to grill fish over a hot fire (see *About Grilling*, 8). Make sure the grill grates are clean and do not use too much oil on the fish (it causes flare-ups). When applicable, start grilling the fish skin side down, then let the skin firm up for a couple of minutes before you try turning the fish (or, if it is a not-too-thick fillet, cover the grill and do not turn it at all). If you lose the skin to the grill rack, do not worry. In fact, cooks who don't like skin find the grill a great way to remove it. A fish grilling basket can make grilling fillets easier.

SERVING SUGGESTIONS

In addition to the recipes here, you can serve almost any simply grilled fish or shellfish with:
- Flavored Butters, 114 to 115
- Salsa Verde, 125
- Vinaigrettes, 110 to 111

Grilled Fillets with Olive Oil and Lemon

4 servings

Use 1-inch-thick firm fish fillets.
Prepare a medium-hot charcoal fire or preheat a gas grill. Make sure the rack is clean and place it about 4 inches from the heat.
Brush:

1½ to 2 pounds fish fillets, with the skin on, rinsed and patted dry

with:

1 tablespoon extra-virgin olive oil
Sprinkle with:

Salt and ground black pepper to taste
Place the fillets skin side down on the grill. Cover the grill if you like; check after 8 minutes. (To check for doneness, see opposite.) Or do not cover the grill and turn the fillets very carefully, with a wide spatula, after no less than 3 minutes. Serve immediately with:

Lemon wedges, several drops of vinegar, or any of the suggested accompaniments above

APPROXIMATE GRILLING TIMES FOR FISH

Food Type	Fire Temperature	Cooking Time (minutes per side)	Or Until
Red snapper, salmon, or striped bass fillets, *1½ inches thick*	Medium	5 to 6	Just opaque throughout
Bluefish fillets, *1½ to 2 inches thick*	Medium	8 to 10	Just opaque throughout
Monkfish, *2 inch chunks*	Medium	7 to 9	Just opaque throughout
Red snapper, whole, *1½ pounds*	Medium	12 to 15	Just opaque throughout
Salmon steaks, *1½ to 2 inches thick*	Medium	9 to 11	Just opaque throughout
Swordfish steaks, *1 inch thick*	Medium	5 to 6	Just opaque throughout
Trout, whole, *10 to 12 ounces*	Medium	5 to 6	Just opaque throughout
Tuna steaks, *2 inches thick*	Medium	4 to 5	Partially opaque but still translucent in center

RULES FOR COOKING FISH

● To cook fish well, all you need to know is that most fish are best treated simply. The Canadian Cooking Theory, a timing technique popularized by the late cooking authority James Beard, advises cooking fish for 10 minutes per inch of thickness regardless of cooking method, cut, or species of fish. This is about as good as generalizations get. But if you follow it religiously, your fish will often be overcooked and occasionally undercooked. (You would never cook a sirloin steak by the clock, would you?)

As a general guideline, 8 to 9 minutes per inch of thickness (1) works a little better than 10—but only as a guideline to be used in tandem with other methods of testing for doneness.

● Timing gives an approximate sense of when a fish is likely to be

done, but you have to check it all the while. Even under the best of circumstances, cooking is inexact. And many things can affect the speed at which fish cooks: the actual temperature of the grill; the shape, thickness, density, and temperature of the flesh; and the presence or absence of marinades or bastes, for example.

● Almost all recipes—including those here—give some timing guidelines for knowing when fish is done. But you will soon learn to recognize the signs of doneness: a firming up of texture; the beginnings of flakiness; an opaque, whiter look throughout.

● In addition, there are two surefire ways to determine whether fish is done: interior appearance and interior temperature. When a fish is opaque throughout, it is done. When you begin to suspect that a piece of fish has nearly finished cooking, take

a thin-bladed knife and gently prod between the flakes of fillets or steaks, or cut between flesh and bone. Do not be afraid to poke fish while it is cooking; if you like your salmon or swordfish just underdone or your tuna medium-rare, learn what it looks like inside (2). Remove the fish from the grill just before it reaches the stage at which you want to eat it; it will finish cooking between grill and plate.

● Just as accurate is an instant-read thermometer (3). Insert it into the thickest part of the fish. All fish is cooked through at 137°F. Usually, 135°F leaves just a hint of translucence and more moisture and is done enough for most people. For tuna and other fish that you might prefer less well-done, try 120°F for starters. Use the knife-peeking technique to double-check the thermometer if you are unsure.

Grilled Swordfish with Tomato-Olive Relish

4 servings

Swordfish adapts easily to strong flavors, like those in the relish (opposite). Start out with a hot grill rack; and don't move the steaks for the first couple of minutes after you put them on the grill.
Mix well in a small bowl:
2 ripe tomatoes, cored and finely diced
1 large red onion, peeled and finely diced
½ cup pitted black olives
¼ cup extra-virgin olive oil
¼ cup fresh lemon juice
¼ cup chopped fresh basil
1 teaspoon minced garlic
Salt and ground black pepper to taste
Set aside. Prepare a medium-hot charcoal fire. Brush:
4 swordfish steaks (10 ounces each), 1 inch thick, rinsed and patted dry
with:
2 tablespoons vegetable oil
Sprinkle with:
Salt and ground black pepper to taste
Place on the grill rack and grill for 5 to 6 minutes per side or until opaque throughout. Serve with the relish.

Grilled Salmon, Tuna, or Swordfish Steaks

4 servings

Fish steaks are a pleasure to grill, because they tend not to stick too much and are easy to turn. Salmon is at its best when still a little translucent inside, and tuna is best a little on the rare side.
Prepare a medium-hot charcoal fire. Make sure the grill rack is clean and place it about 4 inches from the heat on the grill.
Brush:
1½ to 2 pounds fish steaks (2 large or 4 small), at least 1 inch thick, rinsed and patted dry
with:
1 tablespoon extra-virgin olive oil
Sprinkle with:
Salt and ground black pepper to taste
Place on the grill rack and grill until browned, 5 to 6 minutes; turn and grill the other side until browned, 5 to 6 minutes more. (To check for doneness, see page 17.) Serve immediately with:
Lemon wedges, several drops of vinegar, either of the suggested accompaniments on page 118, or *Tart Corn Relish*, 119

Grilled Salmon Steaks with Pickled Corn Relish

4 servings

Salmon can be bought in either steaks or fillets. Both are fine, but the steak (which includes the backbone) is sturdier.
Blanch in boiling water for 1 minute:
2 ears corn, husked and silk removed
Cut off the kernels and set aside in a medium bowl. In a sauté pan over high heat, bring to a boil:
1 cup cider vinegar
½ cup sugar
Remove from the heat and stir in:
½ red bell pepper, seeded and finely diced
½ green bell pepper, seeded and finely diced
½ red onion, peeled and finely diced
Pour mixture over corn and stir in:
2 tablespoons chopped fresh sage
Salt and ground black pepper to taste
Set aside. Prepare a medium-hot charcoal fire. Rub:
4 salmon steaks (10 ounces each), 1 inch thick, rinsed and patted dry
with:
2 tablespoons vegetable oil
Sprinkle with:
Salt and ground black pepper to taste
Place on the grill rack and grill for 8 to 9 minutes per side or until opaque throughout. Serve with the relish.

Teriyaki Grilled Salmon, Tuna, or Swordfish Steaks

4 servings

The secret to really succulent teriyaki is to apply the glaze bit by bit toward the end of the grilling process.

Combine in a small saucepan:

⅔ cup soy sauce
½ cup mirin
1 tablespoon sugar

Cook, stirring, over medium heat until the sugar is dissolved. Increase the heat slightly and cook, stirring occasionally, until foamy. Reduce the heat and simmer, stirring constantly, until the mixture is reduced by half. Let cool, then remove half of it to a glass jar to store in the refrigerator, as the whole recipe makes enough glaze for about 10 servings.

Marinate:

4 salmon or other fish steaks (6 to 8 ounces each), at least 1 inch thick, rinsed and patted dry

in:

1 cup sake

for 15 minutes, turning 2 or 3 times.

Meanwhile, prepare a hot charcoal fire or preheat a gas grill; the fire should be good and hot. Make sure the grill rack is clean and place it about 4 inches from the heat. Remove the fish from the wine and pat dry. Place on the grill rack and sprinkle very lightly with:

Coarse salt

Grill for 2 minutes, until the fish begins to brown. Turn, then grill for 2 minutes more. Move the fish to a cooler part of the grill. Brush the fish with the teriyaki glaze, then grill, with the glaze facing the heat, until the glaze dries, about 1 minute. Brush the other side and grill until the glaze dries. By this time, the fish will be done or nearly so. If it needs another minute, repeat the brushing and cooking procedure once or twice. Serve hot or at room temperature.

Grilled Rare Tuna with Pickled Ginger, Soy Sauce, and Wasabi

4 servings

Prepare a medium-hot charcoal fire. Brush:

4 boneless tuna steaks (8 to 10 ounces each), about 2 inches thick, rinsed and patted dry

with:

¼ cup vegetable oil

Sprinkle with:

Salt and ground black pepper to taste

Place on the grill rack and grill, turning once, 4 to 5 minutes per side for rare, 5 to 7 minutes per side for medium-rare, and 7 to 9 minutes per side for medium. Serve, accompanying each serving with a small dish containing:

2 to 3 tablespoons soy sauce

Pass in separate bowls:

Wasabi paste
Pickled ginger

SAKE, MIRIN, WASABI, AND JAPANESE SOY SAUCE

Sake is the Japanese version of rice wine—any brand of sake is suitable for use in cooking except those labeled "cooking wine," which are made from inferior rice wines and may contain additives. Sake also acts as a tenderizer and removes strong odors in cooking. Substitute pale dry sherry or dry vermouth.

Sometimes called "sweet sake," mirin is rice wine with an 8 percent alcohol content and loads of sugar. Look for *hon-mirin*, which is naturally brewed and contains natural sugars. *Aji-mirin* is sweetened with corn syrup and may contain additives. Store indefinitely on a cool, dark shelf.

Powdered wasabi should be mixed, half and half, with tepid water and then allowed to sit for 15 minutes to develop its flavor. Once the package of wasabi is opened, it deteriorates quickly.

As a rule, Japanese soy sauces (*shoyu*) contain more wheat and are a little sweeter and less salty than Chinese soy sauces. Standard to Japanese cooking is what they call dark soy sauce, which is labeled simply *soy sauce, shoyu,* or *koi-kuchi shoyu*. This sauce, on a Chinese scale of dark to light, would fall on the light end, and in a pinch could be substituted for light soy. The Japanese also market low-sodium soy sauces. Like salt, however, it is better to cut back on the amount of this most fundamental seasoning than to use an altered version of it.

Grilled Salmon Fillets with Lime-Chili Mayonnaise

4 servings

Salmon might be the single most popular eating fish in the United States. Readily available in its farm-raised incarnation, it is sweet and delicate and easy to cook. King, sockeye, and coho are choice wild varieties of salmon, available fresh from spring through fall. Fish labeled "Norwegian" salmon is simply farm-raised Atlantic salmon from Norway. Salmon has the heavy texture needed to hold together during grilling, so it's great on the grill. As always, feel free to use less chili pepper if you don't like your food fiery.

Place in a blender or food processor:

2 egg yolks
2 tablespoons olive oil
2 tablespoons fresh lime juice

With the machine running, add in a steady stream:

¾ plus 2 tablespoons olive oil

Add and pulse to combine:

2 tablespoons chopped fresh cilantro
2 tablespoons ground cumin
1 tablespoon minced fresh chili peppers
1 tablespoon ketchup
1 teaspoon minced garlic
Salt and ground black pepper to taste

Cover and refrigerate. Prepare a medium-hot charcoal fire. Sprinkle:

4 salmon fillets (8 ounces each), rinsed and patted dry

with:

Salt and ground black pepper to taste

Place on the grill rack and grill for 5 to 6 minutes per side or until opaque throughout. Remove and serve with the lime-chili mayonnaise.

LIMES

There are two if not three types of true limes. One group, called the Bartender's lime, is made up of Mexican limes, Key limes, and West Indian limes. They are small and oval. Commercially, they are picked green when they are at their most sour. When they turn yellow-orange, they are mature. Their pulp is pale with a splendidly tart, aromatic flavor. Seedless Bearss limes are larger, the size of a small lemon. For the most flavor, select Bearss when green—ripe, they are greenish yellow inside and out. Their flavor is bright but less intense than that of the Mexican lime group. Some believe Bearss is a separate type, and some regard it as a variety of Persian or Tahitian lime because it is almost identical.

Grilled Salmon with a Chili Spice Rub

5 to 6 servings

This recipe makes enough spice mixture for several dinners. Store it in an airtight container and use it with chicken, beef, and pork, as well as salmon or other meaty fish.

Prepare a hot charcoal fire in a 22½-inch or larger charcoal grill. Stir together in a small nonstick skillet:

¼ cup sweet paprika
1 tablespoon chili powder
1 tablespoon ground cumin
1 teaspoon salt
¼ teaspoon ground cinnamon
¼ teaspoon ground red pepper

Heat, stirring constantly, over medium heat for 2 minutes. Remove from the heat. Pat 2 tablespoons of the spice mixture over the flesh side of:

1 salmon fillet (2½ pounds)

Drizzle over the top:

1½ tablespoons olive oil

When the coals are covered with a thin layer of white ash, push half of the coals to one side of the grill and the other half to the other side so that there are no coals in the center. Place the grill rack over the coals and, with long-handled tongs, rub the grill with a wad of paper towels dipped lightly in:

Vegetable oil

Lay the fillet, flesh side down, over the middle of the grill rack where there are no coals. Cover and grill for 7 minutes. Turn the fillet with two spatulas and grill skin side down for 7 to 8 minutes. (To check for doneness, see page 17.) Remove from the grill with the two spatulas, cut into portions, and serve hot with:

Lime wedges

Grilled Monkfish Skewers with Moroccan Flavors

4 servings

Often overlooked, monkfish is the one pure-white-fleshed fish that always stands up to the grill. Sometimes called "poor man's lobster" because of its wonderfully meaty texture, it can be cooked whole or cut. Monkfish fillets are covered with a thin gray membrane that can be removed with a paring knife.

Rinse, pat dry, and cut into 1- to 1½-inch cubes:

4 to 6 filleted small monkfish tails (about 1½ pounds), fine membrane removed

Combine in a wide bowl:

¼ cup minced fresh cilantro
¼ cup minced onions
1 tablespoon ground cumin
1 teaspoon ground coriander
¼ teaspoon ground cinnamon
Salt and ground black pepper to taste

Moisten with:

¼ cup olive oil

Stir to make a paste. Add the fish and toss to coat well. Refrigerate for up to 2 hours.

When you are ready to cook, prepare a medium-hot charcoal fire or preheat a gas grill. Make sure the grill rack is clean and place it about 4 inches from the heat on the grill. Thread the fish onto 4 metal or wooden skewers (if you use wood, it is best to soak them in water while you marinate the fish), alternating with:

About 24 cherry tomatoes

Do not crowd. Grill the skewers, turning as each side browns and brushing occasionally with any remaining marinade. Total cooking time will be about 12 minutes; monkfish is at its best when all traces of translucence are gone from the center. (To check for doneness, see page 17.)

Grilled Chunks of Swordfish or Other Fish on Skewers

4 servings

Precut chunks of fish may be more or less expensive than fish steaks, depending on whether they are simply cut-up steaks or trimmings. If they are less expensive, fine, but make sure they have not been sitting for too long; the more surface area that is exposed to the air, the faster the fish loses its quality. If you have a thriving rosemary plant, use freshly cut foot-long branches as skewers and omit the herb from the marinade.

Rinse, pat dry, and cut into 1½-inch cubes:

**1½ to 2 pounds thick fish steaks
or fillets**

Whisk together in a large bowl:

¼ cup extra-virgin olive oil
¼ cup fresh lemon or lime juice
**1 teaspoon minced fresh thyme,
  1 tablespoon minced fresh basil,
  or 1 bay leaf, crumbled**
**Salt and ground black pepper
  to taste**

Add the fish and toss to coat well. Let stand.

Prepare a medium-hot charcoal fire or preheat a gas grill. Make sure the grill rack is clean and place it about 4 inches from the heat on the grill. Thread the fish onto 4 metal or wooden skewers (if you use wood, it is best to soak them in water while you marinate the fish); do not crowd. If you like, alternate the fish chunks with:

**Cherry tomatoes, small onion
  wedges, cucumber chunks,
  mushroom slices, and/or other
  vegetables**
Bay or basil leaves

Grill the skewers, turning as each side browns and brushing occasionally with any remaining marinade. Total cooking time will be 10 to 15 minutes; be careful not to overcook salmon, as it will begin to fall from the skewers. (To check for doneness, see page 17). Serve as is or with:

**A vinaigrette or dressing,
  110 to 111**

Grilled Swordfish and Nectarine Skewers

4 servings

Here are fish skewers with a novel touch—nectarines. The result is delightful. Nectarines are peaches in plum clothing. They do not have legendary varieties and, even at their best, they are not as juicy as peaches, but their flavors can be sublime. Either peaches or nectarines work in this recipe. Best with swordfish, these skewers are also good with tuna, mako shark, or halibut.

Rinse, pat dry, and cut into 1½-inch cubes:

**1½ to 2 pounds thick fish steaks or
  fillets**

Whisk together in a small bowl:

½ cup balsamic vinegar
¼ cup fresh lemon juice
1 teaspoon minced garlic
½ teaspoon sugar
**Salt and ground black pepper
  to taste**

Whisk together in a large bowl:

⅓ cup olive oil
⅓ cup coarsely chopped fresh basil
¼ cup fresh lemon juice
1 tablespoon minced garlic
**Salt and ground black pepper
  to taste**

Add the fish to the large bowl and toss to coat well. Add and toss to combine:

**2 nectarines or peaches, pitted,
  quartered, and each quarter
  halved crosswise**
**2 red bell peppers, stemmed,
  seeded, quartered, and each
  quarter halved crosswise**
**2 red onions, cut into 8 wedges
  each**

Prepare a medium-hot charcoal fire or preheat a gas grill. Make sure the grill rack is clean and place it about 4 inches from the heat.

Thread the fish, nectarines, bell peppers, and onions onto 4 metal or wooden skewers (if you use wood, it is best to soak them in water while you marinate the fish); do not crowd. If you have more fresh basil on hand, intersperse a few leaves on the skewers with the other ingredients.

Grill the skewers, turning as each side browns and brushing occasionally with any remaining marinade. Total cooking time will be 10 to 15 minutes. (To check for doneness, see page 17.) Remove from the grill, drizzle the balsamic vinegar mixture over the skewers, and serve immediately.

Grilled Whole Red Snapper

4 servings

A grilled whole fish (opposite) can be a delight to eat but not to cook. To ensure success, begin with a relatively firm-fleshed fish, such as red snapper, pompano, or sea bass.

Prepare a medium-hot charcoal fire or preheat a gas grill. Make sure the grill rack is clean and place it about 4 inches from the heat.

Brush:

2 red snappers or other fish (1½ to 2 pounds each), rinsed inside and out and patted dry

with:

2 tablespoons extra-virgin olive oil

Mix:

2 tablespoons minced fresh parsley or fennel leaves

1 teaspoon coarse salt

Ground black pepper to taste

Rub this mixture all over the fish, inside and out. Place the fish on the grill; cover the grill if possible. Cook, undisturbed, until the side of the fish facing the heat is brown and blistered, about 8 minutes. Turn carefully (do not fret if you lose some of the skin) and cook on the other side until the meat near the bone has lost its translucence, 8 to 10 minutes. (To check for doneness, see page 17.)

To serve, remove the skin from the top of the fish with your hands or a fork. With a thin-bladed knife, make an incision along the back of the fish. Work a spatula or turner under the fillet, gently loosening it from the skeletal structure and removing it completely. Next, lift the whole skeletal structure off the bottom fillet, starting with the tail and holding down the bottom fillet with the knife or the back of a fork. The second fillet is now ready to be served. Serve immediately with:

Lemon wedges, or *Lemon Caper Vinaigrette*, 110

Grilled Whole Red Snapper with Ginger Soy Vinaigrette

4 servings

Prepare a medium-hot charcoal fire or preheat a gas grill. Make sure the grill rack is clean and place it about 4 inches from the heat.

Combine in a bowl:

¼ cup toasted sesame oil

¼ cup peanut or other oil

¼ cup rice or other mild vinegar

¼ cup fresh lime juice

¼ cup soy sauce

4 to 6 dashes hot red pepper sauce

½ cup chopped fresh cilantro

2 tablespoons minced peeled fresh ginger

Salt and ground black pepper to taste

Toast in a small dry skillet over medium-high heat just until the aroma rises:

¾ cup coriander seeds

2 tablespoons red pepper flakes

Pulverize the mixture with the flat side of a heavy knife or coarsely grind in a spice mill. Season with:

Salt and ground black pepper to taste

Rub the spice mixture all over, inside and out:

2 red snappers or other fish (1½ to 2 pounds each), rinsed inside and out and patted dry

Place the fish on the grill; cover the grill if possible. Cook, undisturbed, until the side of the fish facing the heat is brown and blistered, about 8 minutes. Turn carefully and cook until the meat near the bone has lost its translucence, 8 to 10 minutes. Serve immediately with the vinaigrette.

SESAME OIL

In China, sesame oil is considered too expensive to cook with, but it is highly prized as a seasoning sprinkled over dishes just at the end of cooking. In Japan, tempura oil may contain up to one-half sesame oil. The best and most flavorful sesame oil is pressed from seeds that have first been toasted to give them deeper, richer color and taste; oil made from raw seeds cannot compare in flavor. It is best bought in glass bottles or tins because it goes rancid much less quickly than in plastic. Buy a small container, no more than you are likely to use in a short while, and keep for only a month or two in a cool cabinet.

Grilled Whole Mackerel or Trout with Bacon

4 servings

Prepare a medium-hot charcoal fire or preheat a gas grill. Make sure the grill rack is clean and place it about 4 to 6 inches from the heat. Sprinkle:

4 mackerel or trout (1 to 1¼ pounds each), rinsed and patted dry

with:

Salt and ground black pepper to taste

Wrap each fish in:

1 or 2 slices bacon

Place the fish on the grill; cover the grill if possible. Cook, undisturbed, for 3 to 4 minutes, taking care not to burn the bacon (move the fish to a cooler part of the grill if necessary). Turn and continue to cook. Turn again if necessary. The fish is done when the bacon is crisp and there are no longer any traces of blood in the body cavity. Total cooking time will be 12 to 15 minutes. Serve immediately with:

***Corn, Cherry Tomato, and Avocado Salsa*, 116 (opposite)**

Grilled Whole Trout Stuffed with Pesto

4 servings

If you can get your hands on wild trout, they are among the sweetest, richest fish you will ever taste. The farm-raised version, while much less flavorful, is also quite good. Either way, because they are so small, trout are the among the easiest fish to grill whole. Follow the steps in the recipe for Grilled Whole Red Snapper with Ginger Soy Vinaigrette, 24, *to keep the fish from sticking to the grill.*

In a food processor or blender, combine and puree:

1 cup fresh basil leaves
2 cloves garlic
¼ cup toasted pine nuts or walnuts
⅓ cup extra-virgin olive oil
Salt and ground black pepper to taste

Sprinkle:

4 small trout (about 12 ounces each), rinsed and patted dry

with:

Salt and ground black pepper to taste

Place one-quarter of the basil mixture in the body cavity of each trout. Prepare a medium-hot charcoal fire. Place the trout on the grill rack and grill for 4 to 5 minutes per side or until golden brown and blistered on the outside and opaque throughout. Serve at once.

Barbecue-Rubbed Grilled Bluefish with Spicy Tartar Sauce

4 servings

This dish borrows the robust flavors of Southern barbecue in the form of a spice rub. As the fish cooks, the rub forms a dense, flavorful crust on the outside, leaving the inside moist and tender.

Mix well in a medium bowl:

¾ cup mayonnaise
¼ cup chopped fresh parsley
3 tablespoons fresh lime juice
2 tablespoons pickle relish
2 tablespoons Dijon mustard
1 teaspoon minced garlic
4 to 8 dashes hot red pepper sauce
Salt and ground black pepper to taste

Set aside. Combine and mix well in another medium bowl:

¼ cup sweet paprika
¼ cup packed brown sugar
¼ cup ground cumin
¼ cup ground black pepper
¼ cup kosher salt

Rub generously over the outside of:

4 bluefish fillets (8 ounces each), about 1½ to 2 inches thick

Prepare a medium-hot charcoal fire. Place the fillets on the grill rack and grill for 8 to 10 minutes per side or until opaque throughout. Remove and serve at once, accompanied with the spicy tartar sauce.

Grilled Shrimp or Scallops

4 servings

These present no more challenge to the cook than a steak and, as with steak, it is important not to overcook them. Since shrimp and scallops cook in just about the same amount of time and complement each other nicely, you can cook some of each if you like. It is nice to place them on skewers, alternating a shrimp and a scallop. Since scallops have a tendency to stick to the grill, use a thin spatula to loosen them before turning; do not worry about them falling apart. Small bay scallops will not work; look for good-sized sea scallops. Shrimp can be grilled with their shells on or off. See instructions for Peeling and Deveining Shrimp, 31.

Prepare a medium-hot charcoal or wood fire or preheat a gas grill. Make sure the grill rack is clean and place it as close to the heat source as possible. Toss to coat in a shallow bowl:

1½ to 2 pounds sea scallops or large or extra-large shrimp, peeled, deveined if desired
2 tablespoons extra-virgin olive oil
1 tablespoon sherry vinegar or other vinegar (optional)

Grill as close to the heat as possible. Turn the shrimp after the first side becomes pink, 2 minutes or so; turn the scallops when the first side becomes opaque, 2 to 3 minutes. Season liberally with:

Salt and ground black pepper to taste

Grill until the second side is pink or opaque; test one of the pieces by cutting into it to make sure it is cooked through. Serve hot or at room temperature with:

Lemon wedges, minced fresh parsley, and extra-virgin olive oil; or
Scandanavian Mustard-Dill Sauce, **122**

SEA SCALLOPS

These can be quite large but remain tender no matter what the size. Those that are shucked at sea may be soaked in a bath of water and tripolyphosphate; this process extends their shelf life and artificially increases the weight of the meat. Buy unsoaked ("dry") scallops: they taste better, and they brown better (because they contain less water). Be suspicious of sea scallops that are pure white, an indication that they have been soaked; the natural color of sea scallops ranges from white to off-white to pale shades of orange, pink, and tan. Individually quick frozen (IQF) sea scallops can be a good buy and usually retain most of their flavor—sometimes more than older "fresh" scallops.

APPROXIMATE GRILLING TIMES FOR SHELLFISH

Food Type	Fire Temperature	Cooking Time (minutes)	Or Until
Clams, oysters, or mussels	Hot	5 to 7	Until open (discard any that do not open)
Lobster, *about 2 pounds, split*	Medium	Bodies 8 to 10 (1 side only); claws and legs, cracked and covered with pie plate, 5 to 7	Opaque throughout
Sea scallops, *medium, blanched in boiling water for 1 minute*	Hot	2 to 3 per side	Light brown on exterior and opaque in center
Shrimp, *medium peeled*	Medium	3 to 4 per side	Opaque throughout
Squid, *cleaned*	Hot	Tentacles 2½ to 3, rolling around; body 1 to 1½ per side	Tentacles: brown and crispy; bodies: opaque throughout

Grilled Shrimp with Mango-Chili Salsa

4 appetizer servings

Grilled shrimp are a staple of tropical cuisines, their rich flavor providing a perfect match for strong, intensely flavored accompaniments like the salsa in this recipe.

Combine and mix well in a medium bowl:

2 mangoes, pitted, peeled, and diced

½ red bell pepper, seeded and diced

½ large red onion, peeled and diced

2 jalapeño or other fresh chili peppers, coarsely chopped

1 tablespoon coarsely chopped fresh oregano

1 teaspoon ground cumin

6 tablespoons lime juice (about 3 limes)

¼ cup pineapple juice or orange juice

Set aside. Prepare a medium-hot charcoal fire or preheat a gas grill. Sprinkle:

24 medium shrimp, peeled and deveined

with:

3 tablespoons olive oil

Salt and ground black pepper to taste

Thread the shrimp on skewers, place on the grill rack and grill for 3 to 4 minutes per side or until opaque throughout. Remove from the skewers and serve, accompanied with the salsa.

Grilled Shrimp or Scallops, Basque Style

4 servings

Prepare a medium-hot charcoal fire or preheat a gas grill. Make sure the grill rack is clean and place it as close to the heat source as possible. Mix together in a serving bowl:

½ cup fresh lemon juice
⅓ cup extra-virgin olive oil
1 tablespoon minced garlic
¼ to ½ teaspoon hot red pepper sauce, or to taste
½ cup coarsely chopped fresh herbs (any combination of parsley, sage, thyme, basil, marjoram, oregano, chervil, etc.)
Salt and ground black pepper to taste

Toss to coat in a shallow bowl:

1½ to 2 pounds sea scallops or large or extra-large shrimp, peeled, deveined if desired, or a combination
2 tablespoons extra-virgin olive oil

Place on the grill as close to the heat as possible. Turn the shrimp after the first side becomes pink, 2 minutes or so; turn the scallops when the first side becomes opaque, 2 to 3 minutes. Grill until the second side is pink or opaque; test one of the pieces by cutting into it to make sure it is cooked through. Add the hot shellfish to the herb mixture, toss gently, and serve immediately.

Grilled Shrimp or Scallops with Hoisin or Barbecue Sauce

4 servings

Take care not to burn the sauce once you brush it on; if necessary, move the shellfish to a cooler part of the grill.

Combine in a shallow bowl:

1½ to 2 pounds sea scallops or large or extra-large shrimp, peeled, deveined if desired, or a combination
2 tablespoons soy sauce
1 tablespoon sake or white wine

Prepare a medium-hot charcoal fire or preheat a gas grill. Make sure the grill rack is clean and place it about 4 inches from the heat. Remove the shellfish from the soy mixture, pat dry, and place on the grill rack. Grill until beginning to brown, about 2 minutes. Turn, then brush the top side with:

Hoisin sauce or ketchup-based barbecue sauce

Grill for 2 minutes more. Turn again, move the shellfish to a cooler part of the grill, and brush again with sauce. Turn and brush every minute for 3 to 4 minutes, until the shellfish have developed a nice glaze and are cooked through. Serve hot or at room temperature, garnished, if you like, with:

Minced scallions or chopped walnuts

Grilled Shrimp or Scallops with Chili Paste

4 servings

Prepare a medium-hot charcoal fire or preheat a gas grill. Place the grill rack as close to the heat source as possible. Mix in a large, shallow bowl:

1 tablespoon minced garlic

1 tablespoon chili powder (the fresher the better), or to taste

½ teaspoon ground red pepper, or to taste

1 tablespoon peanut or olive oil as needed to make a moist paste

Salt and ground black pepper to taste

Add and toss to coat well:

1½ to 2 pounds sea scallops or large or extra-large shrimp, peeled, deveined if desired, or a combination

Place on the grill as close to the heat as possible. Turn the shrimp after the first side becomes pink, 2 minutes or so; turn the scallops when the first side becomes opaque, 2 to 3 minutes. Grill until the second side is pink or opaque; test one of the pieces by cutting into it to make sure it is cooked through. Serve hot or at room temperature with:

Lime wedges and minced fresh parsley or cilantro, or *Citrus Sauce*, 125

Grilled Shrimp or Scallops with Coconut Curry Sauce

4 servings

Combine in a saucepan:

½ cup unsweetened coconut milk

¼ cup fresh lime juice

1 tablespoon curry powder

1 teaspoon minced peeled fresh ginger

Bring to a boil over high heat, then immediately reduce the heat to low. Simmer, uncovered, for 30 minutes, stirring occasionally.

Meanwhile, prepare a medium-hot charcoal fire or preheat a gas grill. Make sure the grill rack is clean and place it as close to the heat source as possible. Stir into the sauce:

1 teaspoon red pepper flakes, or to taste

Place on the grill as close to the heat as possible:

1½ to 2 pounds sea scallops or large or extra-large shrimp, peeled, deveined if desired, or a combination

Turn the shrimp after the first side becomes pink, 2 minutes or so; turn the scallops when the first side becomes opaque, 2 to 3 minutes. Season liberally with:

Salt and ground black pepper to taste

Grill until the second side is pink or opaque; test one of the pieces by cutting into it to make sure it is cooked through. Remove to a serving bowl, gently warm the coconut sauce if necessary, pour it over the top, and sprinkle with:

2 scallions, minced

1 tablespoon sesame seeds, toasted

PEELING AND DEVEINING SHRIMP

It is best to peel shrimp yourself for two reasons: prepeeled shrimp have lost some of their flavor, and the shells make great stock. If you are grilling, consider cooking shrimp in their shells, for it prevents drying out and helps retain maximum flavor. You should devein shrimp as the vein is actually an intestinal tract and can impart a bitter taste.

If the head of the shrimp is still attached, break it off at the neck.

Peel away the rest of the shell, leaving the tail piece intact.

To remove the vein, make a shallow cut along the back of a peeled shrimp with a paring knife.

Pull out the vein with the tip of the knife.

Grilled Split Lobster with Olive Oil, Garlic, and Lemon

4 servings

Split lobster (opposite) cooks just a little faster than whole lobster, and the smoky flavor of the grill permeates the meat better. Also try whole or split lobster tail.

Prepare a medium-hot charcoal fire or preheat a gas grill. Make sure the grill rack is clean and place it as close to the heat source as possible. Split in half with a knife, *Preparing Lobsters, right:*

4 lobsters (at least 1¼ pounds each)

Having left each lobster attached by a hinge of its shell, remove the head sac and intestines. Crack the claws and legs slightly with the back of a knife. Sprinkle the open bodies and tails with:

Salt and ground black pepper to taste

1 teaspoon to 1 tablespoon red pepper flakes (optional)

Combine in a small bowl:

⅓ cup extra-virgin olive oil

1 tablespoon minced garlic

Brush the lobsters with the oil mixture and place them shell side down on the grill rack. Cover the lobsters with an inverted pie pan or roasting pan. Grill until the flesh is opaque, the tomalley is hot, and any roe is bright orange-red, about 10 minutes. Baste with the remaining oil mixture and serve with:

Minced fresh parsley

Lemon wedges

PREPARING LOBSTERS

All lobsters should be bought alive (and absolutely kicking) or cooked. To kill a lobster before grilling, pierce it behind the head with a sharp, heavy knife. Find the cross-hatch right behind the lobster's head. Plunge the point of a sturdy chef's knife straight down. To avoid muscular contractions, put the lobster in the freezer for a few minutes until it is still. If you wish to halve the lobster, place the cutting board on a baking sheet to collect the juices. Cut forward through the head and back through the body and tail.

Grilled Soft-Shell Crabs

4 servings

Soft-shell crabs are blue crabs that have shed their old shells—they do so in order to grow—and whose new shells have not yet hardened. To grill these delicious creatures, it is best to use a moderately hot fire and keep the grill rack at least 4 inches from the heat source; or use a covered grill and indirect heat.

Prepare a medium-hot charcoal fire or preheat a gas grill. Make sure the grill rack is clean and place it about 4 inches from the heat.

Mix:

3 tablespoons melted butter or olive oil

1 teaspoon minced garlic (optional)

Salt and ground black pepper to taste

Brush the butter mixture over both sides of:

8 soft-shell crabs, cleaned and patted dry

Grill, taking care not to burn the shells (especially the claws), until bright red and firm, 4 to 6 minutes each side. Serve hot with:

Lemon or lime wedges and hot red pepper sauce (optional)

CLEANING SOFT-SHELL CRABS

Although you sometimes can get the fishmonger to do it for you, cleaning a live soft-shell crab is not difficult to do at home. First, snip off the eyes and mouth with a pair of scissors. Then pull back each side of the top shell and pull out and discard the inedible gills. Finally, turn the crab over and pull off the little flap called the "apron." If you purchase frozen soft-shell crabs, keep in mind that they are shipped clean.

Grilled Squid (or Cuttlefish)

4 servings

The instructions for grilling squid (or its close relative, cuttlefish) are the same as those for grilling shrimp or scallops, but the technique is somewhat different. Prepare the hottest fire you can (preferably of hardwood charcoal) and place the grill rack as close to the heat as possible. The idea is to sear the squid before it has a chance to become rubbery.

Prepare a hot charcoal or wood fire or preheat a gas grill. Make sure the grill rack is clean and place it as close to the heat source as possible. Toss to coat in a shallow bowl or baking dish:

2 pounds cleaned squid, tentacles skewered, bodies left intact or skewered

2 tablespoons extra-virgin olive oil

1 tablespoon sherry vinegar or other vinegar (optional)

(Or use any of the flavor treatments suggested for shrimp and scallops, 28 to 31.) When the fire is good and hot, place the squid as close to the heat as possible. Grill about 1 minute, 2 at most, until the surface facing the flame is firm and seared. Turn and cook another 1 to 2 minutes. Be careful—overcooking will make the squid quite tough. Serve immediately with:

Several drops of sherry vinegar, or lemon wedges and minced fresh parsley, or *Salsa Verde,* **125**

Marinated and Grilled Octopus

4 servings

It is necessary to precook the octopus before grilling. Please read the box below.

In a large bowl, combine:

1 octopus (at least 3 pounds), precooked, below

⅓ cup fresh lemon juice

⅓ cup extra-virgin olive oil

1 medium onion, chopped

1 clove garlic, lightly mashed

2 tablespoons minced fresh marjoram, oregano, mint, or basil, or a combination

Refrigerate for 1 to 24 hours. Prepare a medium-hot charcoal fire or preheat a gas grill. Make sure the grill rack is clean and place it as close to the heat source as possible. Cut each of the tentacles from the octopus body and cut the body itself into 2 or 3 pieces. Skewer the pieces if you like or simply place them on the grill. Cook, brushing with the marinade, until beginning to brown and crisp all over, 8 to 15 minutes. Serve hot, at room temperature, or cold, with a drizzling of:

Extra-virgin olive oil

Serve with:

Lemon wedges

PRECOOKING OCTOPUS

Octopus is meaty, tender (when properly cooked), and delicious. Almost always sold cleaned (and often frozen), it only needs to be cooked. Most octopus at the market weigh in at 2 to 3 pounds; look for larger ones if possible, because shrinkage is considerable.

Octopus must be precooked to tenderize it (there are other methods—hurling it against rocks or the kitchen sink, or grating it with radish; but precooking is most reliable). To do so, simmer it in water to cover with 1 tablespoon of salt, 1 bay leaf, 2 crushed garlic cloves, and a few peppercorns. Test for tenderness after 45 minutes by piercing it with a thin-bladed knife; when the knife meets little resistance, the octopus is ready. It may take up to twice that long to become tender, so be patient. Remove from the water, then proceed with the above recipe.

HOW TO CLEAN SQUID

Squid, with its mild, sweet, and nutty flavor, is easy to cook, freezes beautifully, and is in good supply on the East and West Coasts. The trick to cooking is timing. To preserve its tenderness, squid needs to be cooked either quickly over very high heat, as when grilled, or very slowly over low heat, as when braised. Anything in between, and it will be tough and chewy. Cuttlefish, closely related to squid, is widely eaten in Europe and Asia and occasionally makes its way to our markets. Its flavor and texture are similar to those of squid, and it can be prepared in the same way.

1 Grasp the squid's head and innards as far inside the body as you can; pull gently.

2 If the translucent "quill" remains inside, remove it.

3 Using the dull edge of a knife, scrape any remaining innards from the body.

4 Just above the squid's eyes is a hard ball, called the "beak," which creates a slight bulge. Cut the tentacles above that bulge, then squeeze them until the beak pops out. Discard the beak, head, and innards and reserve the tentacles.

5 With your fingers, peel the mottled purple skin off the body and off the tentacles of large squid. Rinse the tentacles and bodies and dry well.

6 The bodies can be sliced into rings, good for most preparations, or left whole to be stuffed. The tentacles can be divided into smaller pieces or left whole.

Mixed Grill of Clams, Oysters, and Mussels

6 appetizer servings

This simple seafood mixed grill is a per-fect way to keep your guests satisfied while you are grilling the main course. As each mollusk comes off the grill, drizzle it with the white wine–butter mixture, sprinkle it with lemon juice and parsley, and hand it to a guest.
Prepare a medium-hot charcoal fire. Place a medium-sized aluminum foil pan on the edge of the grill rack, just barely over the fire, and com-bine in the foil pan:

½ pound butter
½ cup white wine
2 tablespoons minced garlic
7 dashes hot red pepper sauce
Salt and ground black pepper
    to taste
Stir to combine as the butter melts. Meanwhile, place on the grill:
18 littleneck clams, well washed
18 oysters, well washed
50 mussels, well washed and
    debearded, below

Cook until the shells open, 8 to 12 minutes. (Discard any that do not open.) As each clam, oyster, or mus-sel opens, place it in a second foil pan on the edge of the grill rack and pour a bit of the butter-wine mix-ture over each. Serve at once, sprin-kled with a portion of:
1 cup chopped fresh parsley
Juice of 2 lemons

CLAMS, OYSTERS, AND MUSSELS

Hard-shell clams vary more in size and color than in shape or form. But vary they do, from the tiny cockle to the giant sea clam and from the bleached white littlenecks and cherry-stones of the Atlantic coast to the mahogany clam from deeper waters. There is some confusion about the nomenclature of hard-shell clams, but the common names relate prima-rily to size:

Littlenecks are the smallest hard-shell clams, preferably considerably under 2 inches across. They are good eaten raw or cooked. Manila clams are about the same size and are also good raw. In some areas, cherry-stones are 2 to 3 inches across; in others, up to 4 inches. They can still be eaten raw and their flavor is good, but they may be tough. They are excellent for cooking. Mahogany clams are the same size. There are also some excellent varieties that are steely gray, just about blue, in color.

Quahog refers generically to hard-shells as well as to those clams over 3 to 4 inches across. They are too tough for eating raw and too big for eating whole. Cut up and use in soups, stews, and chowders.

Hard-shell clams must be alive (or cooked, canned, or frozen) when you buy them. The smell should be appeal-ing, and the shell should be intact and virtually impossible to pry open. Rinse them a few times. If the shell is very gritty, scrub with a vegetable brush.

There are five species of oysters grown commercially in North America, varying in size, shape, and flavor. Two species are indigenous: the Eastern, which is found from Nova Scotia to Texas, and the tiny Olympia, once plentiful from San Francisco to Washington State and now grown in a few small bays in southern Puget Sound. The European Flat is now raised by growers on both coasts. The Pacific oyster and the small, deep-cupped Kumamoto were brought from Japan to Washington State in the 1920s and in the late 1940s, respec-tively, to replace the Olympia oyster, which was near extinction at the time.

Shells should be tightly closed, impossible to budge. Use a stiff brush and scrub the shells thoroughly, in particular the often-encrusted Eastern and European oysters.

Blue mussels are the most com-mon variety of mussel. New Zealand green-lipped mussels are also good and can be used interchangably. Like clams and oysters, mussels must be alive (or cooked) at the time of pur-chase. The smell should be appealing and the shell intact. Reject any with broken shells or those that seem unusually light or heavy (they may be empty or filled with mud).

Live mussels will close—slowly but surely—when you squeeze or tap the shell.

Remove the "beard," the hairy vegetative growth attached to the shell. You can usually just tug it off or cut it with a knife. Wash the mussels in several changes of cold water. Keep washing until the water runs clear. Discard any with damaged shells.

Put clams, oysters, or mussels in a bowl or mesh bag in the refrigerator, covered lightly with a damp towel. Ice is not necessary. Keep mollusks no more than one day.

ABOUT
GRILLING
POULTRY

*T*he grilling techniques that yield perfect burgers and steaks do not always work for poultry. Burgers and steaks really need nothing more than a red-hot fire, but grilled poultry—with its bones and skin and combination of light and dark meat—requires a more complicated management of heat.

The same hot fire that gives a steak its pleasing brown crust will char bone-in poultry pieces before cooking them through, and the fat dripping onto hot coals will quickly spark an inferno. No wonder so many cooks opt for boneless, skinless poultry breasts—no pesky bones, no fatty skin, no irregular shapes to contend with—but the perks have their price. Both bones and skin add flavor to the meat, and the skin not only protects the meat from the harsh heat but also, when cooked to the proper crispness, adds richness and welcome textural contrast.

Chicken Kebabs, 44

39

Grilling Chicken

Chicken is cooked on an outdoor grill in one of two ways: either directly over the hot charcoals (grilling) or opposite the coals, which are arranged on the grill bottom across from the chicken (grill-roasting or barbecuing). Grilling requires a rather cool fire and an unheated spot on the grill to which the chicken may quickly be pulled in case of flare-ups. It also demands the cook's undivided attention. Grill-roasting is much less bothersome, but it does not crisp and brown the chicken skin, and it imparts a milder flavor and softer, more barbecue-like texture than grilling. For those who want the flavor of grilling and the ease of grill-roasting, a combination of both techniques can be used. The chicken is cooked over moderately hot coals until the skin begins to crisp and render fat; then it is removed to a spot opposite the fire, covered, and allowed to cook through by indirect heat.

Butterflied whole chickens and skin-on chicken parts can be grilled, grill-roasted, or cooked by a combination of techniques. Because of their short cooking time, boneless, skinless chicken parts, whether light or dark meat, should be grilled. (They also benefit from a marinade, which offers the flavor and protection normally provided by the skin.) Whole chickens, however, must be grill-roasted, or they will burn before cooking through.

The recipes in this section are written for use with a charcoal-fired grill, but can be adapted for use with a gas grill (modify the directions to suit your grill and the number of burners). Turn both burners on high to preheat the grill rack (this takes about 10 minutes), then turn off one burner. If grilling, place the chicken on the heated side. If grill-roasting, place the chicken on the unheated side of the rack and cover the grill; the turned-on burner will provide the heat. If the grill is equipped with an upper rack set above the grill rack, turn on both burners and grill-roast on the upper rack.

APPROXIMATE GRILLING TIMES FOR POULTRY

Food Type	Fire Temperature	Cooking Time (minutes)	Or Until
Full chicken breast, *boneless, 10 ounces*	Medium	6 to 8 per side	Opaque with no trace of pink
Half chicken breast, *bone-in, 10 ounces*	Medium-low	10 to 12 per side	Opaque with no trace of pink near bone
Chicken leg, *10 ounces*	Medium-low	15 to 18, rolling around on grill	Opaque with no trace of pink near bone
Chicken thigh, *bone-in, 10 ounces*	Medium-low	8 to 10 per side	Opaque with no trace of pink near bone
Chicken wing	Medium-hot	5, turning occasionally	Opaque with no trace of pink near bone
Duck breast	Low	6 fat side down, 5 to 7 fat side up	Light pink at center
Quail, *butterflied*	Medium-hot	4 to 5 per side	Opaque

Grilled Chicken Dijon

4 servings

Before beginning, please read Grilling Chicken, *opposite.*

Rinse and pat dry:

3½ to 4½ pounds chicken parts

Mix in a large bowl:

⅓ cup olive oil

⅓ cup strained fresh lemon juice

3 tablespoons Dijon mustard

2 to 3 cloves garlic, minced

¾ teaspoon salt

½ teaspoon ground black pepper

Add the chicken pieces to the marinade and turn to coat well. Cover and refrigerate for 2 to 24 hours. Heat 55 to 65 charcoal briquettes until covered with white ash. Spread the coals over one side of the grill to make a medium-hot fire. Replace the grill rack and cover the grill until the rack is hot, about 5 minutes. Place the chicken parts, skin side down, directly over the coals and cook, moving the pieces around as needed to avoid charring, until the skin is crisp and golden, 8 to 10 minutes. Move the chicken opposite the coals and turn skin side up. Cover the grill and cook until the meat is opaque throughout, 10 to 15 minutes more.

Grilled Boneless Chicken Breasts with Peach Chutney

4 servings

Be careful that boneless chicken breasts do not get too done on the exterior before they cook all the way through. If the exterior begins to blacken, move the breasts to an area of the grill where the fire is less intense.

In a sauté pan over medium heat, heat until hot but not smoking:

¼ cup olive oil

Add:

1 red onion, peeled and finely diced

½ red bell pepper, seeded and finely diced

½ green bell pepper, seeded and finely diced

Sauté until the onions are clear, 5 to 7 minutes. Add:

4 ripe peaches, pitted and cubed

1 cup white vinegar

½ cup raisins

½ cup packed brown sugar

Cook for 10 minutes more, stirring. Remove from the heat and stir in:

Pinch of allspice

Salt and ground black pepper to taste

Set aside.

Prepare a medium-hot charcoal fire.

Rub:

4 boneless chicken breasts (10 to 12 ounces each)

with:

About 3 tablespoons vegetable oil

and sprinkle with:

Salt and ground black pepper to taste

Place on the grill rack and grill, skin side down, until the skin is crispy, 8 to 10 minutes. Turn and grill 5 to 6 minutes more or until opaque throughout. Remove and serve with the peach chutney.

Grilled Buffalo Chicken Thighs

4 servings

The spicy chicken wings that originated in Buffalo, New York, have now attained near-legendary snack food status around the country. In this dish, we borrow the flavors of Buffalo wings, but use more substantial thighs as the meat. For the heat, use whatever fresh chili pepper you can most easily get your hands on; the exact amount should be determined by your taste for fiery fare. Feel free to use the same flavoring mixture for grilled chicken wings. Serve with the traditional Blue-Cheese Dressing, right, and crisp celery sticks.

Combine and mix well in a large bowl:

½ cup chopped fresh herbs (any combination of parsley, rosemary, sage, oregano, thyme, and basil)
⅓ cup extra-virgin olive oil
¼ cup red wine vinegar
¼ cup fresh lemon juice
1 tablespoon minced garlic
1 teaspoon to 1 tablespoon minced fresh jalapeño or other fresh chili pepper
10 to 12 dashes of red hot pepper sauce
Salt and ground black pepper to taste

Set aside.
Prepare a medium-low charcoal fire.
Sprinkle:

12 chicken thighs

with:

Salt and ground black pepper to taste

Place on the grill rack, skin side down, and grill for 8 to 10 minutes per side or until opaque throughout. Remove from the grill, add to the bowl of flavoring mixture, toss well, and serve.

Blue-Cheese Dressing

About 2 cups

Puree in a food processor or blender until smooth:

1 cup *Blender Mayonnaise, 113*
½ cup sour cream
¼ cup finely chopped fresh parsley
1 to 2 tablespoons fresh lemon juice or red wine vinegar
1 teaspoon minced garlic
6 dashes of Worcestershire sauce
Salt and ground black pepper to taste
Pinch of ground red pepper

Add and process to the desired consistency:

4 ounces good-quality blue cheese
Taste and adjust the seasonings.
Use or cover and refrigerate.

Extra-Hot Grilled Chipotle Chicken Wings

4 servings

Grilled chicken wings are an excellent snack. Here they are pepped up with a Mexican-inspired sauce featuring the smoky heat of chipotles, which are dried, smoked jalapeños.

Combine and puree in a blender or food processor:

½ cup ketchup
½ cup loosely packed fresh cilantro
4 to 6 tablespoons canned chipotle peppers pureed
2 tablespoons ground cumin
2 cloves garlic, peeled
Juice of 2 limes

Set aside.

Prepare a medium-hot charcoal fire.
Cut at both joints, forming 3 pieces:

20 chicken wings

Reserve the wing tips for stock.
Sprinkle the remaining 2 pieces of each wing with:

Salt and ground black pepper to taste

Place on the grill rack and grill, turning occasionally, until just lightly browned, about 5 minutes. Dunk each wing in the chipotle sauce, return all wings to the grill for 30 seconds, then remove and serve.

CHIPOTLE PEPPERS

Chipotle peppers (dried smoked jalapeños) have an intense, rich, smoky flavor. There are two types of chipotle peppers. The first is the black-red chili chipotle; this small chipotle (1 to 1½ inches long and ½ inch wide) is prized for its sweet, smoky flavor and its dark, rosewood red color. The second type, usually called chipotle meco, is larger (3 to 4 inches long and 1 inch wide) and pale brown, with a more tobacco-like taste.

Chicken Kebabs

8 kebabs; 4 to 6 servings

For the marinade, prepare:
¾ cup *Fresh Herb Vinaigrette*, 110, or
  ***Ginger Soy Vinaigrette*, 111**
Or stir together in a medium bowl:
½ cup olive oil
3 tablespoons strained fresh
  lemon juice
2 to 3 cloves garlic, minced
1 teaspoon salt
1 teaspoon ground black pepper
Pour half of the marinade into
another medium bowl.
Rinse and pat dry, then dip into the
marinade and turn to coat well:
4 boneless, skinless chicken breast
  halves or 6 boneless, skinless
  chicken thighs, cut into
  1-inch cubes
Cover and refrigerate the chicken
for at least 30 minutes or for up to
2 hours. When you are ready to grill
the kebabs, add to the remaining
marinade and turn to coat:
1 large red onion, cut into
  ½-inch chunks
16 small mushrooms

16 cherry tomatoes
1 red, yellow, or green bell pepper,
  cut into 1-inch pieces, or
  2 small zucchini or summer
  squash, halved lengthwise and
  sliced ½ inch thick
Thread the meat and vegetables onto
8 skewers, leaving a little space
between the pieces to allow for even
cooking.
Heat about 50 charcoal briquettes
until covered with white ash. Spread
the coals on one side of the grill to
make a medium-hot fire. Replace the
grill rack and cover the grill until
the rack is hot, about 5 minutes.
Arrange the skewers on the hot rack
opposite the coals and place a strip
of aluminum foil under the exposed
ends of wooden skewers. Grill for 4
minutes, then turn and grill until
the vegetables are crisp-tender and
browned along the edges and the
chicken is opaque in the center, 3 to
4 minutes more.

MAKING CHICKEN KEBABS

Composed of chunks of marinated
boneless, skinless chicken, either
white or dark meat, and an array
of multicolored vegetables, chicken
kebabs are best grilled over a
medium-hot fire. Since vegetables,
generally speaking, cook rather
slowly, cut them in pieces no big-
ger than the chunks of chicken.
Segregating chicken and vegetables
on separate skewers guarantees that
both will be cooked just right,
although this arrangement is less
eye-pleasing. Whatever you do,
thread the chicken and vegetables
on the skewers loosely, for neither
will cook evenly in cramped quar-
ters. If you use two parallel skewers
for each kebab, the pieces will stay
put during grilling, ensuring even
cooking. Remember to soak wooden
or bamboo skewers in water for
at least 30 minutes before use to
prevent them from charring.

Lemon Rosemary Chicken on Skewers

2 to 4 servings

*Cubed chicken breast is marinated,
skewered, then grilled. When grilling the
marinated chicken, make sure to cover
the exposed skewers with foil, or they
will burn. Grilled or sautéed pieces of
fruit or vegetables can be added to the
skewers for color and flavor contrast.
A tasty appetizer, this recipe is easily
doubled.*

Stir together in a medium bowl:
3 tablespoons olive oil

2 tablespoons fresh lemon juice
2 teaspoons grated lemon zest
1 teaspoon chopped fresh
  rosemary
1 teaspoon minced garlic
½ teaspoon salt
¼ teaspoon ground black pepper
Cut into 16 pieces by cutting each
into 8 pieces:
2 boneless, skinless chicken breast
  halves

Add the chicken to the marinade
and stir to coat. Cover and refrigerate
for 1 to 2 hours.
When you are ready to cook,
prepare a medium-hot charcoal grill.
Thread the chicken pieces onto
16 skewers, covering the exposed
wood with aluminum foil. Grill
just until cooked through, about
2 minutes on each side. Serve hot
or at room temperature.

Grilled Chicken Livers with Apple-Bacon Relish

4 servings

Chicken livers are not typically grilled in this country, but they should be. The fire gives the outside of the livers a wonderful, crisp texture while leaving the inside tender. If you can't find Golden Delicious apples for the relish, you may substitute Granny Smiths or McIntoshes.

Place in a large sauté pan:

4 slices bacon, coarsely chopped

Cook over medium-high heat until crisp, about 8 minutes. Remove from the pan and pour off all but about 3 tablespoons of fat. Add:

1 red onion, finely diced

Cook 3 to 4 minutes. Add:

2 Golden Delicious apples, peeled, cored, and finely diced

Cook until tender, 4 to 5 minutes. Add:

½ cup red wine vinegar

2 tablespoons sugar

Cook for 4 minutes more. Remove from the heat and stir in:

¼ cup chopped fresh thyme

1 tablespoon celery seeds

Salt and ground black pepper to taste

Set aside.

Prepare a medium charcoal fire. Rub:

16 chicken livers

with:

3 tablespoons olive oil

3 tablespoons freshly cracked black peppercorns

Salt to taste

Thread the livers onto skewers and grill until crisp on the outside and cooked through, about 4 minutes per side. Remove and serve accompanied with the apple-bacon relish.

Chicken Satay with Peanut Sauce

6 to 8 appetizer servings

Process in a blender until smooth:

½ cup canned unsweetened coconut milk

⅓ cup minced shallots

2 tablespoons brown sugar

2 tablespoons soy sauce

1 tablespoon minced garlic

1 teaspoon ground cumin

1 teaspoon ground coriander

Place in a shallow dish:

1 pound boneless chicken breast, cut into 3 x 1½-inch strips

Add the marinade, toss to coat the chicken strips thoroughly, cover, and let stand for 1 hour at room temperature or refrigerate for up to 24 hours. Prepare a medium-hot charcoal fire. Combine in a medium saucepan:

1 cup canned unsweetened coconut milk

½ cup creamy peanut butter

4 teaspoons firmly packed light brown sugar

1 tablespoon fish sauce

1 tablespoon soy sauce

1 tablespoon canned Thai Massaman curry paste

½ teaspoon curry powder

Whisk in thoroughly:

½ cup hot water

Simmer, stirring occasionally, over low heat until the flavors are well blended, 15 to 20 minutes. Stir in:

2 teaspoons fresh lime juice

Keep warm while you grill the chicken. Thread a 6-inch-long bamboo skewer through each strip of chicken. Lightly brush the skewered chicken on both sides with:

Vegetable oil

Grill, turning once, until golden brown, 3 minutes on each side. Serve immediately, passing the warm peanut sauce on the side for dipping.

MAKING COCONUT MILK

Pour 1 cup boiling water or milk (whole, low fat, or skim) over 1 cup packed fresh coconut shreds. Stir well, cover, and let steep for 30 minutes. To coax every sweet drop from the coconut, process the mixture (no more than 3 cups at a time) in a blender or food processor for 1 minute. Pour all the shreds and milk into a damp clean cloth and press the liquid into a bowl, squeezing until the shreds are dry. This first pressing is referred to as thick coconut milk, and the yield is about 1 cup. A second, even a third and fourth, infusion can be made from the same shreds, but the results will be increasingly thin. For quality's sake, stop at three infusions. Cover, refrigerate, and use within 3 days.

Ash-Roasted Chicken Thighs

3 to 6 servings

In this recipe, chicken thighs are triple-wrapped in aluminum foil and cooked directly on hot coals rather than on a grill rack. On a wintry night, you might try cooking the chicken in your fireplace, burying the chicken in the hot embers surrounding the fire, not directly under it. This recipe can be multiplied to serve as many people as you wish, but wrap only two thighs per packet to guarantee easy handling and even cooking. Using bone-in chicken pieces helps prevent overcooking and keeps the chicken moister and more flavorful. Before beginning, please read Grilling Chicken, 40, *and* Cooking in Ashes, 13. Rinse, pat dry, and remove the skin from:*

6 bone-in chicken thighs

Sprinkle the chicken pieces generously with:

**Salt and ground black pepper
    to taste**

Have ready:

¼ cup minced fresh parsley
6 cloves garlic, thinly sliced
1 lemon, very thinly sliced

Cut a sheet of wide, heavy-duty aluminum foil about 18 inches long. Place 2 thighs in the center of the sheet, sprinkle with parsley and garlic, and top with 2 or 3 lemon slices. Cover with a second sheet of foil, also 18 inches long. Crimp the edges of the 2 sheets to seal securely, then roll the edges in toward the center to make an 8- to 9-inch square packet. Wrap the packet in a third sheet of foil to seal completely. Repeat with the remaining thighs, making 3 packets altogether. Heat 55 to 65 charcoal briquettes until covered with white ash. Push the coals to one side of the grill, arrange the chicken packets in a single layer over the bottom of the grill, and scatter the coals in an even layer over the top of the packets. Cook for 35 minutes. Remove the packets from the coals with tongs and let stand for 10 minutes. Open each packet carefully to avoid being burned by the steam.

Spicy Chicken Hobo Pack with Lime and Chili Peppers

4 servings

Roasting food in the embers of a dying fire is one of the easiest and oldest ways of cooking in the world—and it is still a favorite technique in Boy Scout and Girl Scout camps throughout the United States, where foil-wrapped meals are known as "hobo packs."

Combine in a large bowl and toss well:

**4 bone-in chicken breast halves,
    skin removed**
8 small new potatoes
12 cloves garlic, unpeeled
**⅓ cup chopped fresh cilantro or
    parsley**
¼ cup olive oil
**1 teaspoon minced fresh chili
    peppers**

1 lime, sliced into very thin rounds
**Salt and ground black pepper
    to taste**

Place in the center of a sheet of heavy-duty aluminum foil about 2 feet long. Cover with a second sheet of foil and roll the edges together on all sides to seal. Place in the center of a third length of foil and fold it up around the pack. Prepare a medium-hot charcoal fire. Place the pack on the bottom of the grill and pile coals up on all sides. Cook for 30 to 35 minutes, depending on the intensity of the coals. Remove from the coals, carefully unroll the foil, and serve at once.

JALAPEÑO PEPPERS

These stubby green to red chilies can vary considerably in their heat from totally mild to quite hot varieties found in farmers' markets and their homeland of Veracruz, Mexico. This pepper's bright green, juicy, grassy taste works well in many dishes, from raw salsas to soups and stews, and even stuffed and fried. When mature jalapeños are smoked and dried, they are known as chipotles. Fresh jalapeños measure about 2½ inches in length and ¾ inch wide at the stem end and taper a little before coming to a rather blunt tip.

Grill-Smoked Jamaican Jerk Chicken

6 to 8 servings

Chicken, pork, and fish all can be cooked in the unique Jamaican style known as "jerk." The cornerstone of all jerk dishes is a vinegary, intensely hot paste of dried herbs and habanero peppers or similar Scotch bonnets, which are some five times hotter than jalapeños. If you cannot find these peppers, a habanero-based hot sauce makes a good substitute. Feel free to decrease the quantity of peppers a bit, finding a heat level with which you are comfortable. You can cook the chicken immediately or marinate it, covered and refrigerated, for up to 6 hours. Before beginning, please read Grilling Chicken, 40.

Puree in a food processor or blender:

⅓ cup fresh lime juice
10 fresh habanero or Scotch bonnet peppers, or ¼ cup habanero-based hot sauce
3 scallions, coarsely chopped
2 tablespoons white vinegar
2 tablespoons fresh orange juice
2 tablespoons dried basil
2 tablespoons dried thyme
2 tablespoons yellow mustard seeds or 1 tablespoon dry mustard
2 teaspoons ground allspice
1 teaspoon ground cloves
1 teaspoon salt
1 teaspoon ground black pepper

The mixture should have the consistency of thick tomato sauce. If needed, thin with additional:

Lime juice, vinegar, or orange juice

Rinse and pat dry, then brush this mixture over:

8 whole chicken legs, or 8 bone-in chicken breast halves (with skin)

Prepare a medium-hot charcoal fire. When the coals are covered with white ash, push them over to one side of the grill. Replace the grill rack. Arrange the chicken pieces skin side down opposite the coals. Cover the grill and cook for 20 minutes. Turn the chicken and cook until the meat is opaque throughout and pulls away from the bone, 30 to 60 minutes more, adding more fuel as needed.

Tandoori Chicken

4 servings

In Indian cooking, "tandoori" refers to cut-up chicken, meat kebabs, and flatbreads that are cooked in a tandoor, a fiercely hot, charcoal-fired vertical oven. Before cooking, chicken and meat are marinated in an aromatic mixture of yogurt and spices. (Do not marinate any longer than the time specified in the recipe, or the chicken can turn overly soft and mushy.) This marinade is tinted with a natural dye, which imparts to tandoori chicken its characteristic orange-yellow color. An excellent tandoori-style chicken can be prepared in a covered grill using a very hot fire. To ensure that the outside does not char before the chicken cooks through, use the smallest chicken parts you can find or cut up a 3½-pound chicken into parts. Two split rock Cornish hens also work well. Before beginning, please read Grilling Chicken, 40. *Serve* Fruit Raita, 71, *alongside this spicy dish to help cool down the mouth.*

Raita is best made and served fresh, but it can be prepared ahead and refrigerated for up to 2 hours.

Prepare:

Tandoori Marinade, 106

Remove the skin from:

3½ pounds chicken parts, or 2 split rock Cornish hens

Add the chicken pieces to the marinade, turn to coat well, cover the bowl, and refrigerate for 4 to 6 hours.

Prepare a hot charcoal fire. When the coals are covered with white ash, push them over to one side of the grill. Replace the grill rack and cover the grill until the rack is hot, about 5 minutes. Arrange the chicken bone side down on the hot rack over the coals, cover the grill, and cook for 15 minutes. Turn the chicken and place opposite the coals, replace the grill cover, and cook until the juices run clear when the meat is pricked with a fork, 10 to 15 minutes more. Serve immediately with:

Fruit Raita, 71 (optional)

Grilled Spice-Rubbed Chicken with Lemon and Garlic Oil

4 servings

This recipe calls for bone-in breasts, but mixed chicken parts or boneless, skinless breasts or thighs can be substituted. Since boneless, skinless parts cook more quickly, grill them directly over the coals until completely done, 4 to 5 minutes on each side. If you like, you can omit the spice rub and simply salt the chicken before grilling. Before beginning, please read Grilling Chicken, 40.
Mix:

1½ teaspoons fennel seeds
1½ teaspoons ground coriander
¾ teaspoon dry mustard
¾ teaspoon salt
¼ teaspoon ground cinnamon

¼ teaspoon ground red pepper
Rinse and pat dry, then rub the spice mixture all over:
4 bone-in chicken breast halves (with skin)
Heat 55 to 65 charcoal briquettes until covered with white ash. Spread the coals over one side of the grill to make a medium-hot fire. Replace the grill rack and cover the grill until the rack is hot, about 5 minutes. Place the chicken skin side down over the coals, cover the grill, and cook until the skin is crisp and golden brown, 8 to 10 minutes. Move the chicken to the opposite side of the grill and turn skin side up. Cover the grill and cook until the meat is opaque throughout, 10 to 15 minutes more. Meanwhile, mix in a small bowl:

¼ cup olive oil
¼ cup minced fresh cilantro or parsley, or 1 tablespoon minced fresh thyme or oregano
3 tablespoons strained fresh lemon juice
1 small clove garlic, minced
¼ teaspoon salt
Remove the chicken to a serving platter, spoon the lemon-garlic oil over the pieces, and serve.

Smoke-Roasted Whole Chicken with Garlic and Fresh Herbs

4 to 6 servings

Smoke-roasting the bird on a covered grill adds a whole new dimension of flavor. You can't beat it for a big celebratory family dinner. On a large covered grill, you can cook two 3½-pound chickens without any problem. Any more than that, though, will crowd the grill.

Combine and mix in a small bowl:

2 tablespoons minced garlic
2 tablespoons fresh rosemary
2 tablespoons coarsely chopped fresh parsley
2 tablespoons coarsely chopped fresh thyme or marjoram

Remove the neck and giblets from, then rinse and pat dry:

2 whole chickens (3 to 3½ pounds each)

Rub the outside of the chickens thoroughly with:

¼ cup olive oil
Salt and ground black pepper to taste

Starting at the tip of the breastbone, loosen the skin from the chicken breasts, being careful not to tear the skin. Gently push the garlic-herb mixture under the skin, pushing as far down as possible without ripping the skin.

Prepare a medium-hot charcoal fire in one side of a covered grill. Arrange the chickens on the grill rack opposite the coals. Cover the grill, open the vents about ¼ inch, and cook for 45 minutes. Check the fire every 20 minutes or so, adding more fuel as needed to keep the fire going. After 1½ hours, check for doneness by piercing a chicken thigh with a fork. When the juices run clear, the chicken is done.

Grill-Roasted Whole Turkey

12 servings

It is fun to grill-roast a whole turkey outdoors, and the result is excellent. Turkeys in the range of 11 to 14 pounds work better here than larger ones. You can omit the brining, but this step yields an especially moist, well-seasoned bird and is worth the effort. This method is not recommended for stuffed birds.

Remove the neck and giblets, then rinse and pat dry:

1 turkey (11 to 14 pounds)

In a clean bucket or other container large enough to hold the turkey, mix:

2 pounds salt (2 cups table salt, or 4 cups kosher salt)
2 gallons water

Continue mixing until the salt is dissolved. Submerge the turkey in the solution. If the turkey is not completely covered, prepare additional brine using a ratio of 1 pound salt to 1 gallon water. Set the turkey in a very cool spot for 4 to 6 hours. Remove the turkey from the brine. Thoroughly rinse inside and out, then pat dry the skin and both cavities. Arrange the turkey breast side down on a V-rack or wire rack set inside a large disposable roasting pan. If you are using a flat rack, you may need to prop the turkey up with balls of aluminum foil. Brush the back and legs with:

2 tablespoons melted butter

Pour into the roasting pan:

½ cup water

Open the bottom vents of the grill completely. Ignite about 75 charcoal briquettes and heat until covered with white ash. Divide the coals in half and push half to each side of the grill. Replace the grill rack and set the turkey in the pan between the two piles of coals. Cover the grill and open the cover vents completely. About 40 minutes into roasting, heat another 35 briquettes in a chimney starter. After 1 hour of roasting, remove the turkey from the grill, remove the grill rack, stir up the coals, and add half of the new hot coals to each pile; replace the grill cover. Protecting your hands with paper towels, grasp the turkey at both ends and turn breast side up. Baste the breast with:

2 tablespoons melted butter

If the pan is dry, add more water. Return the turkey to the center of the grill, cover, and cook until a meat thermometer inserted into the thickest part of the thigh registers 175° to 180°F, 60 to 80 minutes more. Remove the turkey to a platter and let stand for at least 20 minutes before serving.

Grilled Rock Cornish Hens in Spicy Port Wine Marinade

4 servings

Rock Cornish hens are a crossbreed of white Plymouth Rock and Cornish strains. Regardless of their lineage, they taste like all other chickens. Rock Cornish hens used to average about 1¼ pounds, a perfect size for an individual serving, but for economic reasons, producers are now bringing them to market in the 1½- to 1¾-pound range. Choose the smallest rock Cornish hens you can find. Cooked whole on the grill, rock Cornish hens will turn out delicious, but they are far easier to handle if you flatten them first even before you marinate them.

Combine in a large, shallow glass baking dish:

2 cups ruby port
½ cup red wine vinegar
¼ cup olive oil

Combine in a mortar or spice grinder and grind coarsely:

2 teaspoons juniper berries
1 teaspoon coriander seeds
1 teaspoon fennel seeds
**1 teaspoon cracked black
  peppercorns**

Add the spices to the dish.
Add:

**1 small onion or 2 scallions,
  coarsely chopped**
3 cloves garlic, lightly crushed
**1 tablespoon peeled minced
  fresh ginger**

Set aside.
Split up the backbone, using a knife

or poultry shears:

4 small rock Cornish hens

Set the hens skin side up on a cutting board and flatten them, using the heel of your hand. (Expect some of the small bones to break in the process.) Place in the dish with the marinade and turn to coat well. Marinate in the refrigerator overnight or, preferably, 2 to 3 days. Turn the hens frequently to distribute the marinade evenly. Remove from the refrigerator ½ hour before grilling, allowing the hens to come to room temperature.

Prepare a medium-hot charcoal fire. If using a covered grill, arrange the hot coals in the center of the fire grate, sides touching. Arrange the hens, skin side down, in a ring around, rather than directly over, the coals. Cover the grill and open the vents completely.

(If using an adjustable or open grill, position the grill rack 3 to 5 inches above the coals. Place the hens directly over the fire. Watch carefully for flare-ups, moving the hens away from the coals if the flames become intense.)

After 10 minutes, turn the hens. (If using a covered grill, move the hens directly over the coals.) Cook 15 minutes more. Turn again, cook for 5 minutes more, and serve.

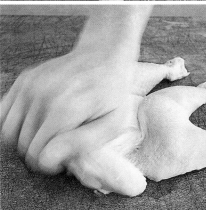

Grilled Duck Breast with Hoisin-Ginger Sauce

4 servings

Duck breast tastes fantastic when grilled, but it does present a special challenge to the griller. It has a high fat content, so as it cooks, fat tends to drip into the fire, causing flare-ups, which can give the duck an ashy flavor. To avoid this, you must watch vigilantly as the duck cooks, moving it around to other areas of the grill as flare-ups occur.

Combine and mix well in a small bowl:

½ cup hoisin sauce
¼ cup rice wine vinegar
1 tablespoon peeled minced fresh ginger

Prepare a very low charcoal fire. Sprinkle:

4 boneless duck breasts (8 to 10 ounces each)

with:

Salt and ground black pepper to taste

Arrange the duck breasts skin side down on the grill rack and grill for about 6 minutes. Move the duck away from flare-ups as they occur. When firm, turn and cook for 5 to 7 minutes more. Remove from the grill, let stand for 10 minutes, then slice thinly on the diagonal. Spoon the sauce over the slices and serve.

RICE VINEGAR AND HOISIN SAUCE

Much of the white rice vinegar produced by Chinese or Japanese manufacturers these days is made from rice wine lees and alcohol. It is pleasant but weaker in flavor than American white vinegars.

Hoisin sauce is brownish in color and made from soybeans. It is almost always sweet, garlicky, and spicy. It has the anise flavor of five-spice powder and is peppered with dried chili.

ABOUT
GRILLING
MEAT

*T*o many dedicated outdoor cooks, meat epitomizes the art of grilling. The robust scents that rise from beef, veal, pork, or lamb; the hearty flavors imparted by the marinade, baste, glaze, or sauce you use; the cross-hatching of grill marks seared into the surface; and the succulence of the meat within all combine to offer unparalleled satisfaction.

As the recipes in this section demonstrate, such tempting results are easy to achieve. Follow the simple guidelines given for each type of meat, paying particular attention to suggested grilling times. To help ensure the best outcome, start with the best ingredients. A good-quality butcher shop or supermarket meat department can provide you with top-notch meats prepared to your order. Keep in mind that well-marbled, tender cuts such as steaks, chops, and tenderloins are those best suited to the high, dry heat of the grill. Avoid excessively thick cuts, which tend to char outside before they are cooked through; two inches should be the thickness limit for individual servings. Cooked quickly and to the degree of doneness recommended in the recipes that follow, the right cuts of meat will guarantee superlative texture and flavor.

Grilled Pork Tenderloin, 68

Grilling Steak

There is no finer treatment for a thick, naturally tender steak than to toss it onto the grill. The high heat of this method delivers the desired crisp, charred exterior while leaving the inside juicy, all with minimal effort and very little time. In the supermarket, look for steaks at least ¾ inch thick. When buying steaks from a butcher, request them cut 2 inches thick for best results. Steaks thinner than ¾ inch tend to dry out and toughen quickly. When grilling, we prefer to cook without a cover, since covering the grill tends to overwhelm the meat with a smoky flavor. The grill rack should be 4 to 6 inches above a bed of luminous coals. For steaks thicker than 1 inch, it is sometimes helpful to shift the steak to a cooler spot on the grill once both sides are well seared if the outside begins to burn before the inside cooks through.

All steaks should be flipped just past the halfway point in the recommended cooking time (see chart, opposite), since the second side will cook a bit faster than the first. For steaks of varying thickness, add or subtract about 1 minute total for every ½-inch difference in thickness. Recommended cooking times are based on steaks straight from the refrigerator. Room-temperature steaks cook a few minutes faster.

Grilled Steak

4 servings

The best cuts for grilling are T-bone, porterhouse, top loin, sirloin, and tenderloin steaks. Cooking times for grilling and broiling are approximate and depend on the many variables of steaks and cooking temperatures. A steak is enhanced easily by the addition of a hot or cold sauce. Consider placing a slice of flavored butter, 114–115, on a hot-off-the-grill steak. The seasoned butter will melt on the way to the table, turning into a quick and savory sauce.

Prepare a medium-hot charcoal fire. Pat dry:

4 small beef steaks (6 to 12 ounces each), or 2 larger steaks (¾ to 1½ pounds each), 1¼ to 2 inches thick

Season both sides with:

Salt and ground black pepper to taste

If desired, rub with the cut side of:

1 clove garlic, halved

Grill the steaks, turning them once just past the halfway point in the cooking time. Consult the chart opposite for cooking times. To check for doneness, make a small incision in the steak and check the center. The interior should be slightly less done than desired. Thicker steaks may require moving the steak to a cooler section of the grill to complete the cooking. Serve with:

A flavored butter or fiery salsa, 114–117

SPICE-CRUSTED SIRLOIN WITH LEMON GARLIC BUTTER

Prepare *Maître d'Hôtel Butter, 114,* adding 1 teaspoon minced garlic. Shape the butter into a cylinder and refrigerate until solid, about 1½ hours. Meanwhile, rub all sides of a 2-inch-thick sirloin steak, 1½ to 2 pounds, with ½ cup *West Indies Dry Rub, 108.* Cook as directed for *Grilled Steak, above.* Serve with the lemon garlic butter.

MARINATED STEAK

Choose from among the marinades on pages 106–107; *Red Wine Marinade* is a good choice. Prepare the marinade and add the steak. Cover and let marinate, refrigerated, for at least 1 hour or up to 24 hours. If using a wet marinade, pat the steak dry with paper towels before cooking. Cook as directed for *Grilled Steak, above.*

APPROXIMATE GRILLING TIMES FOR STEAK

Steak Type	Thickness	Rare (minutes total)	Medium-Rare (minutes total)	Medium (minutes total)
Tenderloin, filet, flank, or skirt steak	1 inch	6 to 8	8 to 10	10 to 12
	2 inches	12 to 14	14 to 18	18 to 20
Boneless top loin, rib, sirloin, top round, or chuck steak	1 inch	6 to 8	8 to 10	10 to 12
	2 inches	16 to 18	18 to 20	20 to 22
Bone-in T-bone, porterhouse, rib, top loin, or sirloin steak	1 inch	10 to 12	12 to 16	16 to 18
	2 inches	18 to 20	20 to 24	24 to 28

CHECKING STEAK FOR DONENESS

The easiest way to check for doneness is to make a small cut in the thickest part of the steak and take a peek at the inside. For bone-in steaks, cut into the meat right near the bone. Some experts claim that cutting into the meat will cause it to leak precious juices. It won't. To check for doneness, pull the steak from the heat when it appears just short of the desired doneness. For example, if you like your steak medium-rare, stop cooking when it still looks somewhat rare inside. Steaks cooked past medium tend to dry out and be tough. A thick steak will continue to cook for a few minutes after you remove it from the heat, and the juices will be redistributed, giving it the perfect degree of doneness.

Black Pepper–Crusted Grilled Sirloin with Red Onion Chutney

4 servings

Steaks need to be at least 1½ inches thick, so they get a nice, strong sear on the outside but still remain rare in the center (opposite). You can crush peppercorns at home with a rolling pin on a cutting board. When shopping for peppercorns, keep in mind that 1 cup peppercorns yields 1 cup cracked.

Heat in a large sauté pan over high heat until very hot:

3 tablespoons olive oil

Reduce the heat to medium and add:

**4 red onions, peeled and
     thinly sliced**

Sauté until deep brown, 8 to 10 minutes. Add:

¼ cup balsamic vinegar
2 tablespoons packed brown sugar
2 tablespoons fresh oregano
**Salt and ground black pepper
     to taste**

Cook for 1 minute, then remove from the heat and set aside. Prepare a hot charcoal fire.

Mix together:

1 cup freshly cracked black pepper
¼ cup kosher salt

Rub this mixture over both sides of:

**4 New York sirloin steaks
     (12 to 16 ounces each), 1½ to
     2 inches thick**

Place the steaks on the grill rack and grill for 5 to 7 minutes per side for rare; 7 to 9 minutes for medium-rare; 10 minutes for medium. Serve with the chutney.

Rib-Eye Steak with Orange-Chipotle Glaze

2 servings

A red-hot hardwood fire is the best way to cook this steak.

Prepare a very hot charcoal fire. Simmer until reduced by almost half:

**1 cup *Orange-Pineapple-Chipotle
     Baste*, 109**

Combine in a small bowl:

**2½ tablespoons cumin seeds,
     preferably toasted**

**2 tablespoons cracked black
     peppercorns**
2 tablespoons kosher salt

Pat dry:

**2 beef rib-eye steaks (6 to 10 ounces
     each), 1 to 1½ inches thick**

Rub the steaks with the spice mixture and grill for 7 to 8 minutes each side for medium-rare. Make a small incision and check the center. The interior should be slightly less done than desired, for it will continue to cook somewhat off the heat. Cook each side for 1 to 2 minutes more for medium. Remove the steak from the heat and let stand for about 5 minutes. Brush with the orange glaze, passing any extra on the side.

Grilled Filet Mignon with Parsley-Chili Sauce

4 servings

Here filet mignon is paired with a version of the spicy parsley sauce typically served with beef in the pampas of South America. This recipe calls for a fair amount of chili pepper in the sauce, so feel free to vary it.

Mix in a small bowl:

½ cup extra-virgin olive oil
¼ cup balsamic vinegar

¼ cup chopped fresh parsley
**2 teaspoons minced fresh chili
     peppers, or to taste**
1 teaspoon minced garlic
**Salt and ground black pepper
     to taste**

Prepare a hot charcoal fire. Sprinkle:

**4 filets mignons (8 to 10 ounces
     each), 2 to 3 inches thick**

with:

**Salt and ground black pepper
     to taste**

Place the steaks on the grill rack and grill for 6 to 8 minutes per side for rare; 8 to 10 minutes for medium-rare; 12 minutes for medium. Serve with the sauce spooned on top.

Grilling Beef Cubes, Strips, and Tips

These dishes are especially popular with those who enjoy the taste of beef but prefer to avoid a large slab of steak. Because the beef in these dishes is cooked quickly over high heat, success depends on starting with naturally tender cuts; no amount of marinating will tenderize a tough cut enough for satisfactory results. Although many markets sell small trays of precubed or sliced

"kebab" or "stir-fry" meat, we recommend buying steaks from the tenderloin, loin, sirloin, or top round and cutting them yourself. Top blade steaks from the chuck are also a good choice as long as you trim out the center line of tough connective tissue. This ensures that you get the high-quality, tender meat you want and often saves money.

Grilled Beef Kebabs

4 servings

Shish kebab originated as a Turkish dish of skewered, marinated lamb grilled over a charcoal fire, but today, we cube and skewer just about anything, from beef to vegetables, and call them kebabs. There is plenty of room for improvisation when assembling kebabs, but combine foods that will cook at the same rate of speed. Quick-cooking, delicate vegetables such as mushrooms and tomatoes are best skewered separately from the meat. Create your own versions by using marinades or basting sauces. If using wooden or bamboo skewers, soak them in water for at least 30 minutes to prevent them from burning. The meat and vegetables are first lightly oiled and seasoned to prevent sticking. As with all tender cuts, beef kebabs should not be cooked beyond medium, or they will become tough and dry.

Cut into 1- to 1½-inch cubes:

1 beef top loin, sirloin, filet, or top round steak (1 to 1½ pounds), 1 inch thick

Mix in a large bowl:

2 tablespoons vegetable oil
1 tablespoon red wine vinegar
2 teaspoons Dijon mustard
1 teaspoon grated lemon zest
1 teaspoon chopped fresh thyme or rosemary, or scant ½ teaspoon dried
1 teaspoon minced garlic
1 teaspoon salt
½ teaspoon ground black pepper

Add the beef along with:

1 medium bell pepper, cut into 1-inch pieces
1 onion, cut into small wedges

Toss to coat the beef and vegetables, cover, and marinate in the refrigerator for 2 to 24 hours.

Prepare a medium-hot charcoal fire. Thread the meat and vegetables on skewers. Grill for 8 to 10 minutes, turning the skewers occasionally. Make a small incision in a cube of meat and check the center. It should be slightly less done than desired, for it will continue to cook somewhat off the heat. Serve immediately.

Herb-Crusted Sirloin Kebabs with Tomato Basil Relish

4 servings

Prepare a very hot charcoal fire.

Combine in a medium bowl:

**2 medium tomatoes, cored and
diced**

**½ cup chopped pitted brine-cured
black olives, preferably
Kalamata**

¼ cup balsamic vinegar

¼ cup olive oil

1 tablespoon minced garlic

½ teaspoon salt

½ teaspoon ground black pepper

Cut into 1½-inch cubes:

**1½ to 2 pounds beef steak,
preferably sirloin tip**

Rub the meat with:

**1 cup *Mediterranean Garlic Herb
Paste*, 108**

Have ready:

**2 small red onions, cut into small
wedges**

**2 bell peppers, preferably
1 red and 1 green, cut into
1-inch pieces**

Thread the meat and vegetables on
8 skewers, evenly distributing the
peppers and onions. Grill for 8 to
10 minutes, turning the skewers
occasionally. Make a small incision
in a cube of meat and check the
center. The interior should be slightly
less done than desired, for it will
continue to cook off the heat. Spoon
the tomato relish onto 4 dinner
plates and top each with 2 kebabs.

Chili-Crusted Flank Steak with Mango Salsa

3 or 4 servings

*This recipe is best with pure ground
chili peppers made from toasted dried
ancho, pasilla, or guajillo peppers, but
ordinary chili powder can also be used.*

Prepare a hot charcoal fire.

Combine in a small bowl:

**2 tablespoons ground dried chili
peppers**

**2 tablespoons cracked black
peppercorns**

1½ tablespoons ground cumin

**1½ tablespoons coarse salt, or
1 tablespoon salt**

Pat dry:

**1 beef flank steak (about
1½ pounds)**

Rub the entire surface of the steak
with the spice mixture and grill
for 4 to 6 minutes each side for
medium-rare. Make a small incision

and check the center. The interior
should be slightly less done than
desired, for it will continue to cook
somewhat off the heat. Cook each
side for 1 to 2 minutes more for
medium. Remove the steak from the
heat and let stand for about 5 minutes. Thinly slice the steak across the
grain. Serve immediately, topped with:

Mango Salsa, 117

Beef Satay with Peanut Sauce

6 to 8 appetizer servings

The sirloin is the hip section between the short loin and the rump. The best cuts come from the top portion of the sirloin and are sold as top sirloin steak, sometimes called top butt steak, hip sirloin, or center-cut sirloin. Be sure to soak the bamboo skewers in water for about 30 minutes before use.

Mix in a blender or food processor until smooth:

½ cup canned unsweetened
   coconut milk
⅓ cup minced shallots
2 tablespoons brown sugar
2 tablespoons soy sauce
1 tablespoon minced garlic
1 teaspoon ground cumin
1 teaspoon ground coriander

Place in a shallow dish:

**1 pound boneless beef sirloin, cut
   across the grain into strips about
   3 x 1½ inches**

Add the marinade, toss to coat the beef strips thoroughly, cover, and let stand for 1 hour at room temperature or refrigerate for up to 24 hours. Prepare a medium-hot charcoal fire.

Combine in a medium saucepan:

**1 cup canned unsweetened
   coconut milk**
½ cup creamy peanut butter
**4 teaspoons firmly packed light
   brown sugar**
1 tablespoon fish sauce
1 tablespoon light or dark soy sauce
**1 tablespoon canned Thai
   Massaman curry paste**
½ teaspoon curry powder

Whisk in thoroughly:

½ cup hot water

Simmer, stirring occasionally, over low heat until the flavors are well blended, 15 to 20 minutes. Stir in:

2 teaspoons fresh lime juice

Keep warm while you grill the meat. Thread a 6-inch-long bamboo skewer through each strip of meat. Lightly brush the skewered meat on both sides with:

Vegetable oil

Grill, turning once, until golden brown, 2 to 3 minutes. Serve immediately, passing the warm peanut sauce on the side for dipping.

FISH SAUCE AND CHINESE SOY SAUCE

Called *nu'o'c ma'm* in Vietnam and *nam pla* in Thailand, fish sauce is made by covering fish, usually anchovies, with brine, and allowing them to ferment in the tropical sun over a period of months. The resulting brown liquid is drained off and used. The first siphoning, from which flows a clear amber liquid, is most highly prized. Fish sauce keeps indefinitely on the shelf.

The Chinese invented soy sauce, and the Japanese learned the technology from them. The Chinese use both light and dark soy sauces. The latter is aged longer and toward the end of the processing is mixed with bead molasses, which gives it a dark caramel hue. Think of them as red and white wines, since as a rule, dark soy sauce flavors (and colors) heartier dishes, whereas light soy sauce is used with lighter dishes.

Grilled Veal Chops

4 servings

If you have an artisinal balsamic vinegar, drizzle a few drops of it on each chop.

Prepare a medium-hot charcoal fire. Pat dry:

4 rib or loin veal chops, 1¼ to 1½ inches thick

Rub the chops with:

2 tablespoons olive oil

Sprinkle with:

Salt and ground black pepper to taste

Place the chops over the hottest area of the grill and sear for 2 minutes on each side. Move the chops to a cooler spot and finish cooking, 8 to 10 minutes, turning halfway through the cooking time. The chops will be well browned and give only slightly when pressed firmly with a finger. Remove to a platter or individual plates and serve with:

Lemon wedges

VEAL CHOPS

Veal chops can be cut from the rib or loin. Rib chops have one curved bone, while loin chops are distinguished by their T-bone shape, with the loin muscle on one side and the tenderloin on the other. Both have a thin layer of fat around the edges. We like to leave at least ¼ inch of fat to keep the chops moist during cooking.

Grilled Filet or Tenderloin of Beef

10 to 12 servings

Those who find filet of beef bland have not tasted it cooked over a charcoal fire. Searing the meat over a hot fire and then pushing the coals to the side, covering the grill, and cooking it over indirect heat give it a deliciously crusty exterior with a tender, moist interior. You can be less fastidious when trimming a tenderloin for grilling, since a little external fat will simply add to the wonderful char-broiled flavor.

Prepare a very hot charcoal fire. Season:

1 filet of beef (about 5 pounds), well trimmed, opposite

with:

1 tablespoon salt

2 teaspoons cracked black peppercorns

Sear the beef well on both sides, about 10 minutes per side. Remove the meat from the grill and push all the coals to one side of the grill. Place the meat on the side without the coals, cover the grill, leaving the vents open a bit, and cook, turning once or twice, until an instant-read thermometer inserted in the thickest part of the meat reads 120° to 125°F for rare, 130° to 135°F for medium-rare, or 140° to 150°F for medium, 25 to 35 minutes (the temperature will continue to rise 5°F off the grill). Remove the beef from the grill, cover loosely with aluminum foil, and let stand for 15 to 20 minutes before carving. Cut the tenderloin into ½-inch slices. If desired, serve with:

Red Onion–Garlic Ketchup, 120, Chimichurri, 122,* or *American Horseradish Cream, 122

SPICE-RUBBED GRILLED FILET OR TENDERLOIN OF BEEF

Prepare Grilled Filet or Tenderloin of Beef, above, substituting for the salt and pepper 1 cup West Indies Dry Rub, 108. Let the filet stand, covered, for up to 1 hour before grilling as directed.

FILET OR TENDERLOIN OF BEEF

The choicest, tenderest cut, known as the filet or tenderloin, is the lean, club-shaped muscle that runs along either side of the backbone, tucked underneath the strip loin and sirloin. The meat from the filet can be utilized in many ways. The whole tenderloin, which weighs 6 to 8 pounds, can be grilled as described at left or easily cut into smaller portions and grilled as loin steaks. For most recipes, figure on 5 to 8 ounces trimmed meat per person. Cooking times vary depending on the size and thickness of the filet. The two constants are never to cook beef filet past medium and to use only dry-heat cooking, such as grilling. A marinade, spice rub, or simply a nicely charred crust are excellent ways to give the very mild meat a flavorful exterior while preserving the tender interior.

HOW TO TRIM AND TIE A WHOLE FILET OR TENDERLOIN OF BEEF

It is easy to trim and tie a whole filet or tenderloin of beef as recommended before grilling.

1 If you buy an entire filet, you will need to do a bit of trimming before cooking by any method. Begin by cutting and pulling away some but not all of the external fat to expose the meat.

2 Some markets leave the long, thin, coarse-grained muscle attached to the side of the filet. This is known as the side muscle or chain muscle; it should be removed (use it in soup or stew), as it is much tougher than the filet.

3 With a sharp, pointed knife, remove the thin, tough, bluish membrane underneath the fat, known as the silver skin. Cut the skin off in long strips, angling the knife away from the filet so as not to cut into the meat.

4 To cook the filet whole, most cooks tuck or trim the thin tail end under the roast and tie it to equalize the thickness. Alternatively, you can simply cut off the 6-inch tail and slice it into strips for use in other recipes.

5 Likewise, the flap of meat at the thick end of the filet can be tied to secure it, or trimmed off and sliced into strips for use in other recipes.

6 In any case, it is best to tie the entire roast with butcher twine, spread at 1½-inch intervals, for an even shape.

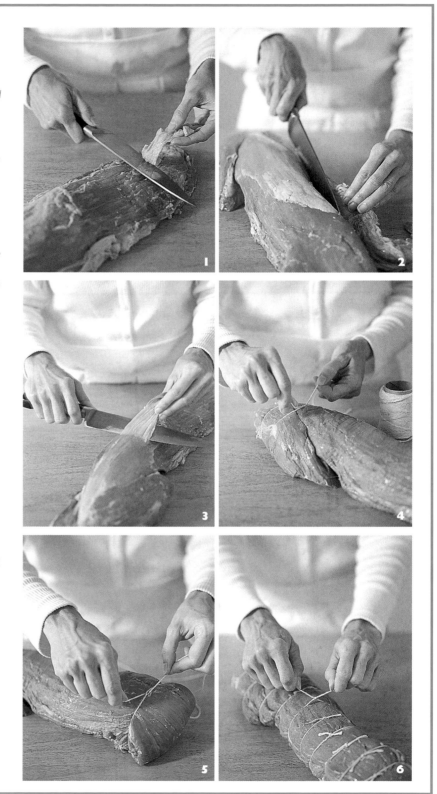

Barbecue-Style Baby Back Ribs

6 appetizer servings

Baby back ribs are much easier to barbecue on a backyard grill than spareribs. Since they are smaller, baby backs easily fit on the portion of the grill rack that is not over any flames. Another advantage is that since baby backs are much more tender than spareribs, the cooking time is considerably shorter; you need only cook the ribs through to add smoky flavor, rather than use the smoke and low heat as tenderizing agents.

Prepare a low charcoal fire in one side of a covered grill. Allow about 40 minutes for the coals to catch completely. If chunks of hardwood are available, place on the coals one at a time once the fire is fully lit.

Rub:

About 1 cup *Southern Dry Rub for Barbecue*, 108

thoroughly over:

2 racks baby back ribs (about 3 pounds)

Arrange the ribs on the grill rack on the side opposite the coals. Cover the grill and open the vents ½ inch. Cook the ribs for 45 minutes, then turn and cook for 45 minutes more, adding more fuel every 15 minutes or so to keep the fire going at a low level. Serve the ribs accompanied with:

***Ray's Mustard Barbecue Sauce*, 109, or *Basic Barbecue Sauce*, 109**

Grilled Five-Spice Ribs

6 to 8 appetizer servings

Peel and discard the rough outside husks, then thinly slice the tender core of:

2 stalks fresh lemongrass

Place in a blender or food processor along with:

3 tablespoons sugar
2 tablespoons chopped shallots
2 tablespoons minced garlic
2 tablespoons fish sauce
2 tablespoons soy sauce
2 tablespoons toasted sesame oil
2 tablespoons peanut oil
2 tablespoons five-spice powder
1 teaspoon chili bean paste

Process until finely pureed, then remove to a large bowl. Add:

3 pounds spareribs or baby back ribs, separated into individual ribs, rinsed, and patted dry

Toss to coat each rib thoroughly. Cover and let stand at room temperature for 1 hour or refrigerate for up to 24 hours.

Prepare a medium-hot charcoal fire. Grill the ribs, turning frequently, about 6 inches from the heat until the ribs are nicely browned and cooked through, 15 to 20 minutes. Serve immediately, sprinkled, if desired, with:

2 tablespoons sesame seeds, toasted

RIBS

Each of the three main types of pork ribs has its devotees. Spareribs come from the side or underbelly of the pig. They have the least amount of meat of the three types but are very flavorful; plan on 1 pound of spareribs per person. The second type, back ribs, are cut from the loin section, or the back, of the pig, and are sometimes called loin back ribs. These are meatier than spareribs and not as fatty. Baby back ribs are simply narrow slabs of back rib cut from the rib end and are sometimes called riblets. A whole rack of back ribs weighs between 1½ and 1¾ pounds; count on 1 pound of back ribs per entrée portion. Last but not least, country-style ribs are the meatiest of all ribs, with much less bone than the other types; they are even sometimes sold boneless. Like back ribs, they are cut from the loin section of the pig. Figure on 8 to 12 ounces of country-style ribs per person.

The two most important factors in cooking ribs well are time—plenty of it—and temperature—very low. On the grill, ribs fare best over indirect heat, with the coals pushed to the sides. Ribs are considered done when you can just loosen, or wiggle, the bone from the meat with little effort and the meat is very tender. Ribs take seasonings well and are delicious sauced or covered with a spice rub. If using a sauce while grilling, baste only during the last 30 minutes of cooking: most sauces contain some type of sugar or sweetener and tend to burn.

Grilled Pork Tenderloin

4 servings

Sauces for grilled tenderloin can be a barbecue sauce, a flavored butter, or a more contemporary dry rub, chutney, dipping sauce, vinaigrette, glaze, or salsa.

Prepare a medium-hot charcoal fire. Pat dry:

2 pork tenderloins (8 to 12 ounces each), left whole or cut crosswise into 1-inch-thick medallions

Rub the tenderloins with:

1 tablespoon olive or other vegetable oil

Season with:

Salt and ground black pepper to taste

Grill the whole tenderloins for 8 to 10 minutes on each side until an instant-read thermometer inserted in the thickest part of the meat reads 150° to 155°F (the temperature will continue to rise 5° to 10° off the grill). Let stand, loosely covered with aluminum foil, for 5 to 10 minutes before slicing. Medallions take about 2 minutes each side.

Season with:

Salt and ground black pepper to taste

If desired, serve with:

Salsa Fresca, 84, or lemon wedges

SPICE-RUBBED GRILLED PORK TENDERLOIN

Prepare Grilled Pork Tenderloin, above, omitting the oil, salt, and pepper. Rub the tenderloin with *Southern Dry Rub for Barbecue, 108,* 2 to 24 hours before you plan to serve it. Refrigerate, covered, until ready to grill.

PORK TENDERLOIN

Pork tenderloin was traditionally sold attached to a bone-in loin roast, hiding beside the backbone. Since the 1980s, though, it has been increasingly available as a separate cut. Tenderloin is very low in fat—nearly as low as skinless chicken breasts—and very tender, with good flavor. It cooks quickly and is best suited to dry-heat techniques such as grilling. Tenderloin can be cooked whole or cut into medallions. Tenderloin is also perfect cut into cubes or strips for kababs or satays. Tenderloins are generally sold pre-packaged with two whole ones in each package. Keep in mind that the best tenderloins are the smaller ones, about 8 to 12 ounces each, generally enough for two servings.

APPROXIMATE GRILLING TIMES FOR PORK

Food Type	Fire Temperature	Cooking Time (minutes per side)	Or Until
Chops, rib or loin, *bone in, 1 inch thick*	Medium-hot	5 to 7	Light pink at center
Cubes, *1 inch in diameter, skewered*	Hot	4 to 6	Light pink at center
Cutlets, *4 ounces each, ¹/₂ inch thick*	Medium-hot	3 to 4	Light pink at center
Tenderloin, *10 to 12 ounces*	Medium	12 to 15, rolling every 3 to 4 minutes	Light pink at center

Grilled Pork Chops

4 servings

For a cool and vibrant accompaniment, try a salsa, relish, or viniagrette, such as Mango Salsa, 117, Red Onion Marmalade, 118, *or* Mojo, 123.
Prepare a medium-hot charcoal fire.
Pat dry:

4 center-cut pork loin chops (bone-in or boneless), ¾ to 1½ inches thick

Rub with:

2 tablespoons olive or other vegetable oil

Season with:

Salt and ground black pepper to taste

Grill over hot coals for 5 to 8 minutes each side for bone-in, or 4 to 6 minutes each side for boneless, depending on thickness. Remove to plates. Serve with the sauce if using.

SPICE-RUBBED GRILLED PORK CHOPS

Prepare *Grilled Pork Chops, above,* omitting the oil, salt, and pepper. Rub the chops with *West Indies Dry Rub, 108,* 2 to 24 hours before you plan to serve them. Refrigerate, covered, until ready to grill.

PORK CHOPS

You can most often expect a pork chop to be a single-serving, thick cut of meat from the pork loin with the bone in—although they may be sold boneless. Pork chops cut from the pork loin have many names. Starting at the shoulder end are pork loin blade chops (also called blade steaks). From the center section come rib chops and loin chops, the latter containing the tenderloin and resembling a T-bone steak. The tenderest pork chops are cut from the center section of the pork loin. After the center section come the sirloin chops, which are larger and sometimes cut thin for a cutlet.

Barbecued Lamb Kebabs

9 skewers

With its pronounced, sweetish flavor, lamb stands up very well to assertive seasonings. These East Indian–style kebabs are molded around the skewers in a sausage shape.

Prepare a medium-hot charcoal fire.
Combine:

1½ pounds lean ground lamb
1 large onion, very finely minced
(about 1 cup)
½ cup chopped fresh cilantro

One 2½-inch piece fresh ginger,
peeled and minced (about ¼ cup)
1 large clove garlic, minced
2 tablespoons chopped fresh mint
2 serrano or jalapeño peppers,
seeded and minced
1 tablespoon ground coriander
1 teaspoon ground red pepper
1 teaspoon salt

Shape the mixture with lightly oiled hands into 9 flattened sausages, about 4 inches long, 1½ inches wide, and 1 inch thick. Carefully thread a skewer through each sausage. Grill until browned and just cooked through, about 2 minutes each side, or broil on a slotted broiling tray for 3 to 5 minutes each side. Serve with:

Pita bread
Fruit Raita, 71

Lamb Brochettes with North African Spices

4 appetizer servings

Keep in mind that the best meat for lamb kebabs is leg meat cut into 1- to 1½-inch cubes.

Prepare a medium-hot charcoal fire.
Mix well:

2 tablespoons caraway seeds
1 tablespoon ground cumin
1½ teaspoons ground coriander
1½ teaspoons ground black pepper

1 teaspoon red pepper flakes, or
to taste
1 teaspoon salt

Thoroughly rub the spice mixture over:

8 ounces boneless leg of lamb, cut
into ½-inch chunks (about
16 cubes)

Thread the lamb onto 4 skewers and grill until the lamb is done to your liking, 5 to 7 minutes each side for medium-well done. Serve warm or at room temperature, accompanied, if desired, with:

Grilled pita wedges
Harissa, 125

Grilled Lamb Skewers with Basil and Lemon

4 servings

This is a version of the classic shish kebab that introduced Americans to the idea of skewer grilling. If you are planning to serve each guest a whole skewer, thread the meat and vegetables sequentially onto the same skewers, which gives a nice appearance. If you plan to unskewer the food before serving, put each item on separate skewer; this gives you a bit more control over the finished product, since the different ingredients might be done at slightly different times.

Mix well in a small bowl:

1 cup chopped fresh basil
¼ cup vegetable oil
4 cloves garlic, minced
Juice of 1 lemon
1 teaspoon red pepper flakes

Place in a large bowl:

2 pounds boneless leg of lamb, cut into 1-inch cubes
3 red onions, peeled and quartered
2 red bell peppers, seeded and cut into eighths

Pour the oil-basil mixture over the lamb, peppers, and onions and toss to coat. Thread the lamb, peppers, and onions onto skewers. Prepare a medium-hot charcoal fire. Place the skewers on the grill rack and grill until the onions and peppers are nicely seared and the lamb is medium-rare, 5 to 7 minutes. Serve at once.

Fruit Raita

Stir together well in a small bowl:

1 ripe banana, peach, or nectarine, finely chopped, or ½ cup fresh pineapple chunks

1 cup yogurt, or ½ cup yogurt and ½ cup sour cream

1 tablespoon golden raisins (optional)

2 tablespoons chopped blanched almonds or macadamia nuts

Up to 4 tablespoons sugar or honey, depending on the tartness of the fruit

Pinch of ground nutmeg or ground cardamom

Grilled Lamb Chops

4 servings

Make sure the chops are close enough to the heat to brown well but not so close that they char; 3 to 4 inches is usually ideal.

Prepare a medium-hot charcoal fire. Pat dry:

8 lamb chops, preferably from the rib or loin, about 1 inch thick

Rub both sides with:

2 tablespoons olive oil

1 teaspoon salt

½ teaspoon ground black pepper

Place the chops on the grill rack and cook for 4½ to 5 minutes each side for medium-rare. Cook the chops for 1 minute more for medium. Remove the chops to a warmed platter or plates and serve immediately. If desired, serve with:

Saffron Garlic Mayonnaise, 113, Anchovy Butter, 114, or Roasted Tomato–Chipotle Salsa, 116

LAMB CHOPS AND STEAKS

The most popular, but expensive, lamb chops are rib and loin chops. Rib chops are recognizable by the "handle" of rib bone extending from the eye of the meat. Loin chops are more compact and somewhat meatier. Chops at least ¾ inch thick are best, as thinner ones are easy to overcook.

Grilled Lamb Chops with Sweet-Sour Apricot Sauce

4 servings

Heat in a sauté pan over medium heat until hot but not smoking:

2 tablespoons vegetable oil

Add:

1 red bell pepper, seeded and finely diced

½ red onion, peeled and finely diced

Sauté for 1 minute. Add:

½ cup dried apricots

½ cup red wine vinegar

¼ cup sugar

Cook for 5 minutes, stirring occasionally. Remove from the heat and stir in:

¼ cup chopped fresh mint

1 teaspoon minced fresh chili peppers

Salt and ground black pepper to taste

Set aside. Prepare a medium-hot charcoal fire.

Sprinkle:

8 loin lamb chops, 1½ to 2 inches thick

with:

Salt and ground black pepper to taste

Place on the grill and grill for 6 to 7 minutes each side for medium-rare. Serve at once, accompanied with the apricot sauce.

Grilled Lamb Steaks

4 servings

Whisk together:

¾ cup olive oil

½ cup dry red wine

1 teaspoon salt

½ teaspoon ground black pepper

Pour the mixture over:

2 pounds lamb steaks or shoulder chops, about ¾ inch thick

Cover and marinate in the refrigerator for at least 1 hour or up to 24 hours.

Prepare a medium-hot charcoal fire. Place the meat on the grill rack and cook for 3 to 4 minutes each side for medium-rare. Cook for 1 minute more for medium. Remove the steaks to a warmed platter or plates and serve immediately. If desired, serve with:

Tapenade, 124, or Anchovy Butter, 114

GRILLED LAMB STEAKS WITH MEDITERRANEAN GARLIC HERB PASTE

Prepare as for Grilled Lamb Steaks, left, omitting the marinade and, instead, rubbing the steaks with 1½ cups Mediterranean Garlic Herb Paste, 108. Marinate and grill as directed.

Grilled Butterflied Leg of Lamb

8 to 10 servings

Pat dry:

1 butterflied leg of lamb (4 to 5 pounds), trimmed to an even thickness of 2 to 2½ inches

Rub the entire surface with:

½ cup *West Indies Dry Rub,* 108

or a mixture of:

3 tablespoons minced fresh rose-mary, or 1 tablespoon dried

2 tablespoons minced garlic

1 teaspoon salt

1 teaspoon ground black pepper

Marinate in the refrigerator for at least 1 hour or up to 24 hours. Prepare a medium-hot charcoal fire.

To cook, place the lamb skinned side down on the grill rack. Cook until well seared on the outside but still juicy and pink on the inside, about 12 minutes each side. Cook for a few minutes more each side for medium. Let the lamb stand for 6 to 8 minutes, loosely covered with aluminum foil, then cut into ½-inch-thick slices. Serve immediately with, if desired:

Red Onion Marmalade, 118

Roasted Tomato-Chipotle Salsa, 116

MARINATED BUTTERFLIED LEG OF LAMB

Before preparing *Grilled Butterflied Leg of Lamb, left,* marinate the butterflied meat, lightly covered, in the refrigerator for 6 hours in 1½ tablespoons olive oil, 1 cup dry red wine, 1 tablespoon grated lemon zest, 2 crumbled bay leaves, 2 crushed cloves garlic, and 2 tea-spoons dried oregano. Pat the but-terflied leg of lamb dry before grilling as directed.

APPROXIMATE GRILLING TIMES FOR LAMB

Food Type	Fire Temperature	Cooking Time (minutes per side)	Or Until
Chops, *bone-in, 1½ to 2 inches thick*	Medium-hot	6 to 7 for medium rare	Center color as desired
Cubes, *about 1 inch*	Medium-hot	5 for medium rare	Center color as desired
Leg, *4 to 5 pounds, boned and butterflied, about 2½ inches thick*	Hot	Seared over coals, 4 to 5 minutes per side; cooked opposite coals, 15 to 20 minutes total for medium rare	Center color as desired

HOW TO BUTTERFLY A LEG OF LAMB

A butterflied leg of lamb is completely boned and then spread flat and trimmed, making it ideal for quick grilling, much like a large steak. Most butchers will butterfly a leg of lamb for you, but it is a straightforward task you can perform yourself. Figure on 6 to 8 ounces boneless meat per person.

1 Butchers often roll boneless legs of lamb and secure them with butcher twine.

2 Lay the boneless leg flat and cut away the kneecap, the small white disk of cartilage that is found toward the shank end of the meat.

3 Carefully trim away any lumps of fat and sinew.

4 Even out the thickness of the meat by making lengthwise cuts about 1 inch deep in the thicker sections of the meat and spreading them open like a book (or butterfly).

5 The butterflied leg should be approximately the same thickness— 2 to 2½ inches—all over. The flat side of a meat mallet or the bottom of a small, heavy pan can be used to further flatten any thicker portions.

6 For a neat presentation and ease in flipping the meat on a grill, run 2 or 3 skewers crosswise through the meat to secure any loose flaps. After cooking, carve a butterflied leg of lamb by slicing it on the diagonal in ¼- to ½-inch slices much as you would carve a steak.

ABOUT GRILLING **BURGERS,** SANDWICHES & PIZZAS

*A*s widespread and varied as enthusiasm for outdoor cooking may be, many cooks still fire up the grill for one reason and one reason alone: to cook hamburgers or hot dogs on a nice summer day. This chapter devotes itself to the needs of those cooks, providing as it does strategies for grilling burgers and frankfurters perfectly and embellishing them in many different ways.

But the following pages do more besides. They recognize that, even for simple sandwiches, the grill provides an opportunity for endless creativity. From slices of grilled crusty bread topped with sliced steak and tomatoes and served open-faced to warm tortillas wrapped around well-seasoned and quickly grilled seafood or meat, even the most casually eaten and served dishes gain extra dimensions of pleasure when prepared over a live fire.

Grilled Open-Faced Steak Sandwich with Quick Pickled Onions, 84

The Hamburger

4 burgers

The hamburger gets its name from the German city of Hamburg, where the idea of eating raw shredded beef (steak tartare) is said to have been introduced by sailors returning from Russia. Some enterprising Hamburger apparently got the idea of cooking the delicacy—and the next thing anyone knew, fast-food burgers were being sold on the Champs-Elysées. (The first American appearance of the burger is, not surprisingly, a matter of some debate, but many historians trace it to St. Louis, Missouri, which has a large German-derived population, in 1904.) It is a mistake to make burgers with lean beef, for they need some fat for flavor and moistness. The ideal burger meat is 100 percent ground chuck, with about 20 percent fat.

Mix together in a large bowl with your hands or a wooden spoon:

1¼ pounds ground chuck
Salt and ground black pepper to taste

Divide the meat into 4 equal portions and form each into a burger about 1 inch thick. Cook, flipping once, by grilling over a hot fire, about 3 minutes each side for rare, 4 minutes each side for medium, and 5 minutes each side for well-done. Place the burgers between:

4 hamburger rolls or other rolls, halved, or 8 slices bread of your choice

Add your choice of:

Tomato ketchup or other ketchup of your choice, 120
Green Tomato Relish, **118**
Mustard

Serve at once.

GROUND BEEF

By far the most popular ground meat in America is ground beef. Different cuts contain varying levels of fat. Ground chuck has the best flavor and is the best for hamburgers. Look for pale red or pink meat; too red meat may have been falsely colored. While extremely lean meat may appeal to our health-consciousness, it is important to note that a little fat is necessary to prevent the meat from drying out and becoming overcooked. Conversely, very pale pink meat is often high in fat and will literally shrink and cook away. Untreated ground beef will naturally darken with exposure to light, but this darkening is not harmful. Ground beef should smell fresh, not sour, and should be moist but not slimy. Do not store any uncooked ground meat for more than 24 hours.

CHEESEBURGER

Prepare *The Hamburger, opposite,* topping each burger, after flipping it, with 1 or 2 thin slices of American cheese, aged Cheddar, or other cheese of your choice. For a Bacon Cheeseburger, top each cooked cheeseburger with 2 or 3 crisp cooked slices bacon, cut crosswise in half.

CALIFORNIA BURGER

Prepare *The Hamburger, opposite.* On each bun, place 1 thin slice of red onion. Top with the cooked burger, then with a thick slice of ripe tomato and a leaf or two of Boston lettuce or other mild lettuce of your choice, and a slice of avocado.

DOUBLE-CHEESE TOMATO BURGER

Prepare *The Hamburger, opposite,* topping the burgers, after flipping them, with 1½ cups grated Gruyère cheese, 2 sliced ripe plum tomatoes, and 2 tablespoons grated Parmesan cheese. Before serving, sprinkle each burger with 1 tablespoon minced fresh parsley.

BLUE CHEESE AND BACON BURGER

Applewood-smoked bacon is a delight on these burgers.
Prepare *The Hamburger, opposite,* topping the burgers, after flipping them, with four 1-ounce slices Saga or other blue cheese and 4 crisp cooked slices bacon, cut crosswise in half.

TEX-MEX BURGER

Prepare *The Hamburger, opposite,* adding several dashes of hot red pepper sauce to the meat before shaping the burgers. Serve the cooked burgers topped with guacamole and *Salsa Fresca, 84.*

CHILI BURGER

Prepare *The Hamburger, opposite,* topping each cooked burger with several tablespoons of the chili of your choice and about 2 teaspoons minced onions.

BARBECUE BURGER

Prepare *The Hamburger, opposite,* topping each cooked burger with 1 to 2 tablespoons of barbecue sauce, 109.

Grilled Becker Burgers

4 burgers

The traditional way of serving these burgers in the Becker home is as open-faced sandwiches on grilled whole-wheat bread.

Mix together in a large bowl:

1 ½ pounds lean ground beef
Ground black pepper
2 tablespoons soy sauce
2 tablespoons port
Several drops hot red pepper sauce

Divide into 4 equal portions and form each into a burger about ¾ inch thick. Cook, flipping once, by grilling over a hot fire, about 4 minutes each side for medium-rare. Serve at once on grilled whole-wheat bread.

Chutney Turkey Burger

4 burgers

For the simplest turkey burgers, shape a pound of ground turkey into 4 patties, season to taste with salt and pepper, then grill and serve on a bun with thick slices of red onion. For added moisture and flavor, we suggest combining the meat with other ingredients.

Stir together in a small bowl:

½ cup tomato chutney or mango chutney, large pieces chopped
1 tablespoon Dijon mustard
2 teaspoons fresh lemon juice, or to taste

Combine in another bowl:

1 pound ground turkey
3 tablespoons mango chutney, large pieces chopped
2 scallions, minced
1 teaspoon ground cumin
1 teaspoon ground coriander
Salt and ground black pepper to taste

Shape into 4 patties and grill, turning once, just until cooked through, 4 to 5 minutes each side.

Meanwhile, spread the chutney mixture over:

8 thick (½-inch) slices sourdough bread, toasted

Top 4 slices of the bread with:

Arugula leaves
4 very thin slices red onion

Place the burgers on top, top with the remaining bread, and serve hot.

Mushroom Burger

4 burgers

The rich, earthy flavor of mushrooms and onions sautéed in butter adds a great new dimension to a classic burger. Although you can use fresh shiitake, cremini, or portobello mushrooms, regular white button mushrooms work fine.

Heat in a large skillet over medium heat:

2 tablespoons butter

Add:

2 small onions, sliced

Cook, stirring, for 5 minutes. Add:

8 ounces mushrooms, wiped clean and sliced
1 yellow or red bell pepper, diced (optional)
1 teaspoon fresh thyme leaves
Salt and ground black pepper to taste

Cook, stirring, for 10 minutes. Keep warm while you prepare:

The Hamburger, 78

Top the cooked burgers with the mushroom mixture.

MUSHROOMS

Shiitakes are umbrella shaped and brown. Cultivated on logs, they have a distinctive earthy taste. Creminis, or Italian browns, are button mushrooms grown outdoors, with a naturally more developed flavor. Portobellos are cultivated mushrooms, full-blown creminis. They are generous in size (up to 6 inches wide).

The Hot Dog

4 hot dogs

An American beach and backyard grill classic, hot dogs can be dressed up with a variety of add-ons or eaten with your favorite condiments. Since they are precooked, all you need to do is heat them up. For a reduced-fat hot dog, use chicken or turkey frankfurters and do not butter the buns.

Spread each of:
4 hot dog buns, toasted if desired with:
2 teaspoons butter (8 teaspoons total)
Grill until well seared, about 3 minutes each side:
4 frankfurters

Place on the prepared buns. Add your choice of:
Ketchup
***Green Tomato Relish*, 118**
***Tart Corn Relish*, 119**
Mustard
Chopped red or white onions
Serve at once.

BARBECUE DOG

Top each hot dog with 1 to 2 tablespoons of barbecue sauce of your choice.

GERMAN DOG

Top each hot dog with 3 tablespoons prepared sauerkraut.

CHILI DOG

Top each hot dog with ¼ cup chili.

MEXICAN DOG

Add as little or as much chopped jalapeño pepper as you desire.
Top each hot dog with 2 tablespoons *Salsa Fresca, 84*, ½ jalapeño pepper, coarsely chopped, and 1 tablespoon grated Monterey Jack cheese.

CHEESE DOG

Top each hot dog with 1 or 2 slices of American cheese or 2 tablespoons of cheese spread.

CHILI CHEESE DOG

Use as few or as many toppings in this recipe as desired. Also, amounts of each topping can be varied. Cheddar cheese can be used in place of American.
Top each hot dog with ¼ cup chili, 2 tablespoons cooked kidney beans, 2 tablespoons chopped onions, 2 tablespoons shredded American cheese, and a pinch of ground red pepper.

North Carolina Pork Barbecue Sandwich

12 to 15 servings

As close as you can get to making authentic North Carolina pulled pork barbecue in your backyard, this fork-tender meat is at its best on white rolls, topped or served with a classic cole slaw. The key, as with all barbecue, is to keep the temperature of the fire low and to be patient, cooking the meat slowly enough so the tough collagen within the pork butts is dissolved and the meat becomes fully permeated with smoke. If you like beer and lazy chat, this recipe is for you. It not only allows you but actually requires you to hang out by the grill, boasting about your barbecue prowess and sipping beers, for about five to seven hours.
Rub:

About 1 cup *Southern Dry Rub for Barbecue,* 108
thoroughly over:
2 boneless pork butts (4 to 5 pounds each)
Prepare a low charcoal fire in one side of a covered grill. Allow about 40 minutes for the coals to catch. If chunks of hardwood are available, place on the coals one at a time once the fire is fully lit.
Place the pork on the grill rack on the side opposite the coals. Cover the grill and open the vents ½ inch. Cook the pork for 5 to 7 hours until tender, adding more fuel every 30 to 40 minutes to keep the fire just smoldering.

While the meat is cooking, combine in a large bowl:
1 cup white vinegar
1 cup cider vinegar
1 tablespoon sugar
1 tablespoon red pepper flakes
1 tablespoon hot red pepper sauce
Salt and black ground black pepper to taste
Remove the meat from the grill and chop or shred it. Add the vinegar sauce to taste, mix well, and pile onto:
Soft white rolls
Top with:
Cole Slaw, below

Cole Slaw

6 servings

Two basic recipes for an American favorite; improvisations on the theme are encouraged.
For a creamy version, stir together until well blended:
¾ cup *Blender Mayonnaise, 113*
¼ cup white vinegar
1 tablespoon sugar
Alternatively, prepare:
½ to 1 cup *Basic Vinaigrette, 110,* or other vinaigrette of your choice, 111
Finely shred or chop:
1 small head chilled green or red cabbage, cored and outer leaves removed

Stir in just enough dressing to moisten the cabbage. Season with:
Salt and ground black pepper to taste
If desired, add any of the following:
Dill, caraway, or celery seeds, or a combination
Chopped fresh parsley, chives, or other herb
Crumbled crisp bacon
Pineapple chunks
Grated peeled carrots
Coarsely chopped onions, bell peppers, or pickles
Stir again and serve immediately.

Grilled Steak Fajitas

4 servings

Fajitas (opposite) were little known outside Texas until not very long ago.
Arrange in a single layer in a nonreactive roasting pan just large enough to hold it:

1 skirt steak (about 1¼ pounds), cut across the grain on the bias into 1-inch-wide strips

Whisk together:

¼ cup lime juice (about 1½ limes)
2 scallions, minced
3 cloves garlic, minced
3 tablespoons minced fresh cilantro
1 tablespoon vegetable oil
½ to 1 teaspoon red pepper flakes
¼ teaspoon ground coriander or cumin
¼ teaspoon ground anise seeds

Pour the marinade over the steak, turn to coat, cover, and refrigerate for 12 to 24 hours, tossing several times.
Prepare a medium-hot charcoal fire. Remove the steak from the marinade, discarding the marinade, and season with:

½ teaspoon salt

Grill until it is cooked to your liking, 2 to 3 minutes each side for medium-rare. Meanwhile, wrap in aluminum foil:

Four 7-inch flour tortillas

Place off to one side of the grill until heated through, about 4 minutes. Unwrap the tortillas and top each one with the steak, along with a spoonful or two of:

***Salsa Fresca*, right**

Roll up the tortillas and serve hot.

Salsa Fresca

About 2 cups

Combine in a medium bowl:
½ small white or red onion, or 8 slender scallions, finely chopped, rinsed, and drained
2 tablespoons fresh lime juice
Add to the onions:
3 to 5 ripe plum tomatoes, seeded and finely diced
¼ to ½ cup chopped fresh cilantro
3 to 5 serrano or fresh jalapeño peppers, seeded and minced
6 radishes, finely diced (optional)
1 medium clove garlic, minced
Stir together well. Season with:
¼ teaspoon salt, or to taste

Grilled Open-Faced Steak Sandwich with Quick Pickled Onions

4 servings

A tri-tip sirloin is a less expensive cut that makes remarkable steak sandwiches, especially when the beef and bread are grilled over a charcoal fire.
Prepare and set aside:

Quick Red Onion Pickle, 119

Build an extra-large charcoal fire and, before grilling, spread the fire so that one side of the grill is very hot and the other side is not hot at all. The very hot side should be so hot that you can hold your hand 6 inches above the coals for only 3 seconds. You should be able to hold your hand over the cooler side for twice as long. Pat dry:

1 beef tri-tip roast (1½ to 2 pounds) or 1½- to 2-inch-thick top round or sirloin steak, excess fat/membrane trimmed

Rub the entire surface of the meat with:

¼ cup *Southern Dry Rub for Barbecue*, 108

Sear the meat on the very hot side of the grill for 3 to 4 minutes each side. Move it to the cooler side of the grill and cook each side for 8 to 10 minutes more for medium-rare. Make a small incision and check the center. The interior should be slightly less done than desired, for it will continue to cook somewhat off the heat. Cook each side for 1 to 2 minutes more for medium. Remove the steak from the grill and let stand, loosely covered, for 5 minutes. Meanwhile, grill over the cooler side of the grill until lightly toasted, about 2 minutes each side:

4 slices crusty white bread

Thinly slice the steak, about ¼ inch thick, across the grain. If desired, spread each slice of bread with:

***Red Onion–Garlic Ketchup*, 120**

Place the steak slices on the toast. Top with the pickled onions and serve immediately.

Grilled Fish Tacos

4 to 6 servings

Use your favorite firm fish in this delicious version of an American favorite.
Place in a shallow baking dish just large enough to hold them in a single layer:

2 pounds swordfish, halibut, monkfish, or other firm fish, cut into 1-inch cubes (24 pieces)

Mix well:

⅓ cup fresh sour orange juice or lime juice

3 tablespoons coarsely chopped fresh cilantro or oregano

1 to 2 tablespoons minced jalapeños or other fresh chili peppers

1 teaspoon salt

1 teaspoon ground black pepper

Pour the marinade over the fish, cover, and refrigerate for at least 1 hour or up to 3 hours.
Prepare a medium-hot charcoal fire.
Have ready:

12 corn tortillas

If using fresh tortillas, warm them 1 at a time in a skillet over medium heat, flipping them once or twice, for about 15 seconds; wrap in a dish towel and keep warm in a 250°F oven. If using store-bought tortillas, wrap them in a dish towel, place in a steamer over simmering water, cover, and steam for 1 minute. Turn off the heat and let stand in the covered steamer for 20 minutes.
Meanwhile, remove the fish from the marinade and thread it onto skewers. If using wooden skewers, soak in water for 30 minutes, and cover the ends with foil. Grill over the hot fire, turning once, until the fish is opaque in the center, 4 to 5 minutes each side. Remove from the heat and slide the fish off the skewers onto a platter. Place on the table with:

2 cups shredded romaine lettuce, washed and dried

1 cup thinly sliced radishes

Corn, Cherry Tomato, and Avocado Salsa, 116

Place the warmed tortillas in a basket and serve immediately, allowing each guest to layer ingredients into his or her own taco as desired. Or layer each tortilla with the fish, lettuce, radishes, and a generous dollop of the salsa, fold up, and serve 2 to 3 to each guest.

GRILLED SHRIMP TACOS

Prepare Grilled Fish Tacos, above, substituting 1½ pounds medium shrimp, shelled and deveined, for the fish. Grill the shrimp until opaque in the center, 3 to 4 minutes each side. Serve with the corn tortillas, 2 cups shredded cabbage, and *Roasted Tomato– Chipotle Salsa, 116.*

Bruschetta with Tomatoes and Basil

8 slices

From the Italian word meaning "roasted over coals," bruschetta is the original garlic bread. In its simplest form, it is nothing more than grilled country bread rubbed with garlic cloves and brushed with olive oil. (The Tuscans call it fett'unta, *meaning "under oil.") Bruschetta can also serve as the foundation for a wide variety of toppings, however. A single bruschetta makes a good appetizer, while two or three will make a nice lunch when accompanied with a simple salad. If you follow the same process with smaller pieces of bread, you will be making crostini, or little toasts, which are traditionally served as appetizers.*

Prepare a medium-hot charcoal fire. Place on the grill:

8 thick slices crusty firm Italian bread or other country-style bread

Grill, turning once, until golden brown, about 3 minutes each side. Remove from the heat and rub the surface with:

2 large cloves garlic, halved

Brush with:

3 to 4 tablespoons extra-virgin olive oil

Combine well:

4 medium, ripe tomatoes, cored and diced

½ cup slivered fresh basil leaves

Salt and ground black pepper to taste

Divide the tomato mixture among the bruschetta and serve immediately.

BRUSCHETTA WITH MOZZARELLA AND FRESH OREGANO

Premium mozzarella, a cow's milk cheese, is always fresh and kept in a liquid bath. It has a creamy center and tastes of fresh milk with a little tang. If fresh mozzarella is impossible to find, use the low-moisture mozzarella found in most supermarkets. Grill the bread, rub with garlic, and brush with oil as directed for *Bruschetta with Tomatoes and Basil*, above. Top each slice with shredded mozzarella cheese (about 8 ounces total). Broil just until the cheese is bubbling. Top with diced fresh tomatoes (about 1 large tomato total) and chopped fresh oregano (about 2 tablespoons total).

BASIL AND OREGANO

Sweet basils combine oils also in anise, orange blossoms, and lilacs. Spicy basils have red stems and green leaves brushed with purple. Lemon basil is in a class of its own. The blend of lemon and basil just may be the most brilliant marriage of flavors in all herb leaves. Keep in mind that basil complements tomatoes and blends well with garlic and thyme. Peppery with a hint of mint and clove, basil's flavor becomes more intense during cooking.

Oregano is a member of the mint family. It is often confused with marjoram, but oregano has an earthier flavor. Its leaves are medium green and somewhat heart shaped, from ¼ to 1½ inches long. Of the numerous varieties, Greek oregano sets the standard.

Grilled Pizza with Anchovy and Mozzarella

One 10- to 12-inch pizza

On the grill, the pizza comes into direct contact with fire. The smoke curls around the dough, leaving its delicate perfume on the surface. This recipe serves four as an appetizer or one as a main course. The dough can easily be doubled or tripled.

Combine in a mixing bowl or in the bowl of a heavy-duty mixer:

1 teaspoon active dry yeast

2 tablespoons warm (105° to 115°F) water

Let stand until the yeast is dissolved and the water is foamy on the surface, about 5 minutes. Add:

⅔ cup cool water

2 cups unbleached all-purpose flour

1½ teaspoons coarse salt

Mix until the dough comes together. Knead by hand or with the dough hook on medium speed until the dough is smooth and elastic, about 10 minutes. Brush a large bowl with:

Olive oil

Add the dough and brush the surface with:

Olive oil

Cover the bowl with plastic wrap and let rise in a warm place away from drafts until doubled in volume, about 2 hours. Punch the dough down. Cover with plastic wrap and let rise for at least 45 minutes at room temperature or overnight in the refrigerator.

While the dough is rising, prepare the filling. Rinse in warm water, pat dry with paper towels, and coarsely chop:

3 anchovy fillets

Combine with:

3 tablespoons olive oil

Set aside.

Prepare a hot charcoal fire, setting the grill rack 3 to 4 inches above the coals. Brush one side of a large baking sheet with:

1 tablespoon olive oil

Place the ball of dough on the pan and turn it over to coat with oil. With your hands, spread and flatten the pizza dough into a 10- to 12-inch freeform circle, ¼ inch thick. You may end up with a rectangle rather than a circle; the shape is unimportant. If the dough shrinks back into itself, let it stand for a few minutes, then continue to spread and flatten the dough. Do not make a lip. Take care not to stretch the dough so thin that it tears. If this happens, all is not lost; rather than try to repair the holes, simply avoid them when adding the toppings. When the fire is hot (you will be able to hold your hand 5 inches above the fire for only 3 to 4 seconds), use your fingertips to lift the dough gently by the 2 corners closest to you and drape it onto the coolest part of the grill rack. Catch the loose edge on the grill first and guide the remaining dough into place over the fire. Cover, and within 2 to 3 minutes, the dough will puff slightly, the underside will stiffen, and grill marks will appear. Using spring-loaded tongs and a spatula, immediately flip the crust over onto the coolest part of the grill. Quickly brush the grilled surface with a liberal amount of the anchovy oil. Spread over the entire surface of the pizza:

3-inch ball of fresh mozzarella, thinly sliced and patted dry on paper towels

1 tablespoon chopped fresh mint

1 tablespoon chopped fresh parsley

Sprinkle with the remaining anchovy oil.

After the toppings have been added, slide the pizza back toward the hot coals so that about half of the pizza is directly over the heat. Rotate the pizza frequently so that different sections receive high heat, and check the underside by lifting the edge with tongs to be sure it is not burning. The pizza is done when the top is bubbling and the cheese is melted. Serve immediately.

ANCHOVIES

When fresh, anchovies are often confused with sardines and herring; no matter, they are all pretty much interchangeable. They have a soft, delicate texture, a rather strong flavor, and dark colored flesh. They are sold fresh, packed in salt, and packed in oil. When fresh, anchovies need to be deboned like sardines. When packed in salt, you'll need to rinse and pick over them; when in oil, rinse if you wish and reserve the oil for use in cooking. When salted or canned, use anchovies as flavoring in other dishes; when fresh, grill them with excellent results. Keep in mind that despite their strong flavor, fresh anchovies are moderate to low in fat. Be sure to brush with some oil before grilling.

RULES FOR GRILLING PIZZA

● To grill pizza successfully, you will need patience and extra dough to master the technique.

● For the dough, use an all-purpose unbleached flour. It has the right amount of gluten to produce a dough that stretches easily.

● Grilling pizza requires a hot fire started with kindling and fueled with hardwood charcoal. Build your fire on one side of the grill.

● For cooking, you will want a cool area on the grill in order to add the toppings without burning the bottom of the crust.

● If you have a hibachi, build the fire on one side.

● For kettle-type grills, create a center line with two or three bricks laid end to end and bank the charcoal on one side.

● A large grill is more convenient than a small one, but if your grill cannot accommodate a 12-inch round of dough, simply divide the dough and make 2 or 3 small pizzas.

● Set up your work area as close to the grill as possible. The dough, olive oil, and a variety of topping ingredients should be close at hand and ready before you begin.

● The crispy, chewy texture of the grilled pizza comes from the irregularity of the dough stretched by hand rather than with a rolling pin.

● When you transfer the dough from the work surface to the grill, it has a tendency to stretch and sag a bit, so it is a good idea to work very close to the grill.

● When choosing toppings, keep in mind that less is more. If the ingredients on top are too thick, the dough will burn before the top has a chance to cook.

● The pizza should cook in 5 to 8 minutes. If after 8 minutes the cheese is not melted and the toppings are not bubbling, either your fire is not hot enough or you have placed an excess of ingredients on top. If so, remove from the grill and finish under your broiler.

OLIVE OIL

Olive oil is refined with solvents or chemicals, which are steamed off. The best grades of olive oil are made simply: the fruit is crushed and the oil collected. Buy the freshest olive oil possible. Pressing is done from midautumn to January, depending upon origin. Usually these oils reach the market by early spring. Store in a cool, dark place and use within 1 year. Keep oil away from heat and light.

ABOUT GRILLING **VEGETABLES** & FRUITS

Vegetables are usually halved or sliced for grilling to speed up cooking, and the cut surfaces need to be coated with oil or a vinaigrette, which will protect against drying and also promote browning. The popular practice of cooking aluminum foil—wrapped packets of cut-up vegetables on the grill is actually a form of steaming and works with any vegetable that steams well, although carrots and other hard vegetables can take twice as long as they would were they steamed on the stove.

The grill gives a luscious outdoor flavor to fruits, and it is easy to fit pieces on the grill around whatever meat, poultry, or fish is also cooking. Small pieces of fruit should be threaded on skewers so they do not fall through the slats. When skewering, cut the pieces so that all will finish cooking at the same time—soft fruits in larger chunks, firm fruits in smaller ones.

Grilled Ratatouille Salad, 98

Easy Grilled Vegetables

For campfires and backyard barbecues, here are two simple ways to cook vegetables.

METHOD 1:

Use frozen or sliced and washed vegetables. Place them on heavy-weight aluminum foil and seal them. Cook the foil-wrapped vegetables on a grill, or under (or on) hot coals, for 10 to 15 minutes.

METHOD 2:

Place thick slices of tomatoes, mushrooms, peppers, or parboiled onions directly on a greased grill rack above the coals. Cover with an inverted colander and cook until tender.

Grilled Corn on the Cob

There are many ways to grill corn on the cob. All methods use a low fire, and all can be used for any number of ears of corn.

METHOD 1:

Peel back the husks only far enough to remove the silk, then wrap the husks back around the ears of corn. Soak in water for 30 minutes to 1 hour. Place on the grill rack and grill, turning a few times to cook evenly, 15 to 30 minutes or until tender.

Advantage: Tender corn.

Disadvantage: Corn cooks mainly by steaming, gets little smoky flavor.

METHOD 2:

Follow method 1, but grill for 20 minutes, then remove the husks, return the corn to the grill, and cook for 5 minutes more, directly over the coals, rolling frequently.

Advantage: Smoky flavor.

Disadvantage: Corn can dry out.

METHOD 3:

Do not remove husks or silk from the ears of corn. Place on the grill rack and grill, turning a few times to cook evenly, about 30 minutes.

Advantage: Smoky flavor, easy.

Disadvantage: Husks and silk must be removed after cooking.

APPROXIMATE GRILLING TIMES FOR VEGETABLES

Food Type	Fire Temperature	Cooking Time (minutes per side)	Or Until
Bell peppers	Medium-hot	3 to 4	Nicely browned
Corn on the cob, *husks intact*	Medium	About 25, rolling often	Kernels are golden brown
Eggplant, *cut lengthwise into slices*	Medium	4 to 5	Golden brown
Fennel bulb, *sliced into wedges*	Medium	3 to 4	Seared and soft
Mushrooms	Medium	8 to 10	Golden brown
Onions, *quartered*	Medium-hot	4 to 5	Golden brown
Potatoes, baking, *cut into 1/2-inch slices and blanched for 8 to 10 minutes*	Medium	7 to 9	Well browned
Scallions	Medium	4 to 5	White ends are golden brown
Tomatoes, *halved*	Low	6 to 9	Lightly browned
Zucchini or summer squash	Medium	4 to 5	Tender and golden brown

Grilled Sweet Onions

4 servings

Sweet onions are mostly grown during the winter in warm climates. They are full-size but do not keep well. Sweet onions also tend to be juicy, and their moisture content adds to their perishablility. Vidalias, Granos, Branexes, and Mauis all fall into the sweet onion category. Sometimes sweet onions are referred to as slicing onions. Large red onions can be used when sweet onions are unavailable. Select only firm, crisp, unblemished onions and store in perforated plastic vegetable bags in the refrigerator crisper.

Prepare a medium-hot charcoal fire. Prepare:

3 large Vidalia or other sweet onions, peeled and sliced into 1-inch-thick rounds

Thread the slices onto skewers so they do not fall apart. Rub with:

¼ cup olive oil

Salt and ground black pepper to taste

Place the onion slices on the grill rack and grill until nicely browned, about 6 minutes each side. Remove from the grill and remove the skewers. Serve plain or with:

Fresh Herb Vinaigrette, 110, Garlic Mayonnaise, 113, or Chili Butter, 115

Grilled Leeks

4 servings

If you have very thin leeks, leave them whole but split them lengthwise two-thirds of the way down to wash them.

Prepare a medium-hot charcoal fire. Trim the dark green leaves, halve lengthwise, thoroughly wash, and pat dry:

4 medium leeks (white part only)

Place cut sides up on a platter and brush with:

Olive oil

Make sure the oil gets into the inside of the leaves. Season with:

Salt and ground black pepper to taste

Grill the leeks, cut side facing the heat, until lightly browned, about 7 minutes. Turn them over once and grill for a few minutes more. The exact time will depend on the heat of the fire—just take care not to burn them. When done, remove to a platter and season with any one of the following:

Extra-virgin olive oil and finely minced fresh parsley or tarragon

Mustard Butter, 115

Basic Vinaigrette or French Dressing, 110

Green Goddess Dressing, 111

WASHING LEEKS

The layers of a leek can contain dirt, since the white stalks are buried in the ground. Swish julienned or sliced leeks in a large bowl of cool water. Let them stand a few minutes while the dirt falls to the bottom, then lift them out. Repeat if there is a lot of dirt left in the bowl. If you are using leeks that are halved lengthwise, soak them in water for 15 minutes, swish them around, and rinse under cool water, fanning the leaves open as you rinse.

Grilled Sesame Scallions

4 servings

The most common fresh onions are scallions, called green onions in most parts of the country. They are essentially seedling onions, long, slender, and supple. Scallions are available year-round. They can also be broiled in a baking pan until browned on both sides.

Prepare a medium-hot charcoal fire. Trim the root ends and leave 5 inches of green on:

16 scallions

Rub with:

2 tablespoons toasted sesame oil

Salt and ground black pepper to taste

Place on the grill rack and grill, turning several times, until golden brown, 3 to 5 minutes.

Grilled Red Bell Peppers and Red Onions

4 servings

Prepare a medium-hot charcoal fire.
Prepare:

2 red bell peppers, halved lengthwise and seeded

2 small red onions, trimmed and halved crosswise

Brush with:

¼ cup olive oil

Sprinkle with:

Salt and ground black pepper to taste

Place on the grill rack and grill until well browned, about 5 minutes each side. Remove and let stand until cool enough to handle. Cut the peppers into ½-inch-thick slices and separate the onion rings. Toss in a large bowl along with:

¼ cup extra-virgin olive oil

¼ cup balsamic vinegar

¼ cup coarsely chopped fresh parsley

1 teaspoon minced garlic

Salt and ground black pepper to taste

Serve immediately.

Grilled Green Tomatoes

6 servings

Green tomatoes grill beautifully.
Prepare a medium-hot charcoal fire. Combine in a shallow bowl and set aside:

2 cups fine cornmeal
½ cup all-purpose flour
1 tablespoon chopped fresh parsley
1 tablespoon chopped fresh thyme
1 teaspoon paprika
⅛ teaspoon ground red pepper
    (optional)
Salt and ground black pepper
    to taste

Cut into ½-inch-thick slices:

6 large green tomatoes
Brush all over with:
Olive or other vegetable oil
Coat with the cornmeal mixture. Grease the grill rack and add the tomatoes. Grill, turning once with tongs, just until they begin to soften, 4 to 6 minutes. Serve hot, plain or with:
Blender Mayonnaise, 113
with:
2 to 3 tablespoons minced fresh
    tarragon
stirred in.

Grilled Tomato Soup

About 4 cups

A rustic-style, intensely flavored soup that is delicious either hot or cold. The grilling brings out the sweetness of the tomato as well as adding a light smoky flavor. The soup may thicken more when it is cold than when it is hot. If thinning is desired, add a little more stock or a bit of water.

Prepare a medium-hot charcoal fire. Halve through the circumference and seed:

3 pounds ripe tomatoes
Brush both sides with:
Olive oil, preferably extra virgin
Carefully grill the tomatoes on both sides until slightly charred, 6 to 9 minutes per side. Remove to a platter. Heat in a soup pot, over medium-low heat:

2 tablespoons olive oil, preferably
    extra virgin
Add:
1 medium onion, coarsely chopped
Cook, stirring often, until tender but not brown, 5 to 10 minutes. Add the tomatoes and stir, breaking up the tomatoes with the spoon. Stir in:

1 cup chicken stock
1 tablespoon dry white wine
1 clove garlic, minced
Simmer until the tomatoes are softened and have released their juices, 25 to 30 minutes. Puree until smooth. Strain, if you wish, to remove the skin. Stir in:

¾ teaspoon salt
¼ teaspoon ground black pepper
Let cool to room temperature and refrigerate until cold. Just before serving, stir in:

2 tablespoons fresh lemon juice
2 tablespoons chopped fresh basil
1 teaspoon balsamic vinegar
Adjust the seasonings, ladle into bowls, and garnish with:

1 sprig fresh basil
1 thin slice lemon, seeded
    (optional)

Simple Grilled Tomato Sauce

4 servings

This sauce is not cooked to blend the flavors, but simply mixed together after the tomatoes, onions, and garlic have been grilled. It is excellent over pasta.

Rub:

6 medium tomatoes, cored and cut into slices about 1 inch thick

2 small red onions, peeled and cut into slices about 1 inch thick

with:

¼ cup olive oil

Salt and ground black pepper to taste

Prepare a medium-hot charcoal fire. Place the onion and tomato slices on the grill and cook until nicely charred, 3 to 4 minutes per side. Meanwhile, place on skewers and grill until browned, 2 to 3 minutes:

10 cloves garlic, peeled and blanched for 90 seconds

Remove the tomatoes, onions, and garlic from the grill, chop coarsely, and place in a large bowl. Toss together with:

1 cup coarsely chopped fresh basil

⅓ cup extra-virgin olive oil

Salt and ground black pepper to taste

Grilled Fennel and Tomatoes with Black Olives and Basil

4 servings

Prepare a medium-hot charcoal fire. Rub:

2 fennel bulbs, trimmed and cut lengthwise into ½-inch-thick wedges

4 plum tomatoes, halved

with:

¼ cup olive oil

Salt and ground black pepper to taste

Place on the grill and cook until the tomatoes are nicely browned and the fennel is slightly soft, 3 to 4 minutes each side. Remove from the grill and place in a large bowl along with:

½ cup coarsely chopped pitted imported black olives

⅓ cup coarsely chopped fresh basil

¼ cup extra-virgin olive oil

Juice of 1 lemon

Salt and ground black pepper to taste

Toss lightly and serve at once.

FENNEL

A bulb of fennel looks like a bunch of celery with a wide, round base. The individual stalks are broad and thin, while the tops are round and fleshy. The flavor of the whole plant is like licorice. Select sparkling white bulbs with crisp, bright greens. Store in a perforated plastic bag in the refrigerator crisper.

Grilled Ratatouille Salad

6 servings

Prepare a medium-hot charcoal fire. Combine in a bowl:

2 to 4 tablespoons olive oil

2 to 3 tablespoons red wine vinegar, to taste

When the coals are covered with gray ash, coat with the oil mixture:

Twelve ½-inch-thick eggplant slices

3 slender leeks (white part only), split down to the root ends and washed thoroughly

4 plum tomatoes

2 fennel bulbs, quartered lengthwise

2 medium zucchini, cut lengthwise into thick slices

3 red or yellow bell peppers

½ head garlic, unpeeled

Grill the vegetables, turning as needed, until the tomatoes and peppers are charred on the outside and the other vegetables are tender, about 5 minutes for the zucchini, up to 20 minutes for the garlic. Remove from the grill and let cool slightly. Peel, seed, and dice the tomatoes and bell peppers. Dice the fennel and zucchini into ½-inch pieces.

Trim the root ends from the leeks and slice. Squeeze the garlic from the skins and mash. Combine the vegetables, except the eggplant, in a bowl. Just before serving, stir in:

3 tablespoons minced fresh basil

1 tablespoon extra-virgin olive oil

Pinch of grated orange zest

Salt and ground black pepper to taste

Arrange the eggplant slices on a platter, top with the ratatouille, and serve at room temperature.

Grilled Eggplant Planks with Feta, Raisins, and Pine Nuts

4 servings

Eggplant can be simply put on the grill whole (be sure to pierce the skin) and, when it has turned almost black and collapsed like a paper bag, its flesh can be scooped out and used dozens of ways. A quicker way to grill it, though, is to cut it lengthwise into planks and place the planks directly on the grill. In a medium bowl, combine, gently toss, and set aside:

½ cup crumbled feta cheese

¼ cup raisins

¼ cup toasted pine nuts

¼ cup roughly chopped fresh oregano

¼ cup olive oil

Cut lengthwise into planks about 1 inch thick:

2 medium eggplants

Rub cut sides of planks with:

½ cup olive oil

Salt and ground black pepper to taste

Prepare a medium-hot fire. Place the eggplant on the grill and grill until the eggplant is golden brown and soft, 4 to 5 minutes per side. Remove from the grill and serve, liberally sprinkled with the feta mixture.

EGGPLANTS

Eggplants may be available year-round, but their peak season is midsummer to midautumn. Select eggplants of whatever sort that are heavy for their size, with taut skin, a fresh, green cap and stem, and not a single soft spot, cut, or bruise. In standard and Asian types, the skin should be glossy (Thai eggplants have a matte finish). As a rule, small to medium eggplants are the choicest, being the youngest. Store unwrapped in a cool place or in a perforated plastic bag in the refrigerator crisper. Be careful not to bruise eggplant, for its skin can be fragile. Standard and Asian eggplants can be used interchangeably in recipes. All eggplants are tasty grilled. Bear in mind that eggplant discolors when cut with a carbon-steel knife, so use a stainless-steel one. Also, make sure you use non-reactive bowls.

Grilled Mushrooms

6 first-course servings

The best mushrooms for grilling are portobello, shiitake, and oyster.

Prepare a medium-hot charcoal fire. Wipe clean and remove the stems from:

6 large portobello or 12 large shiitake mushrooms

Brush both sides with:

Olive oil

Season with:

Salt and ground black pepper to taste

Place the mushrooms stem side up on the grill rack and grill, turning once, until seared and tender, 5 to 8 minutes each side. Place on a large platter and garnish with:

6 sprigs flat-leaf parsley, chopped

Grill to toast:

6 or 12 thick slices Italian bread

Rub with:

2 cloves garlic, halved

Brush lightly with:

Olive oil

Place the toast around the platter to soak up the mushroom juices, or place 1 large mushroom on each slice of toast.

GRILLED MUSHROOMS WITH GARLIC BUTTER

Cooking with flavored butters is an easy way to add interest to the simplest of foods. Here a garlic-infused blend adds gutsy flavor to grilled mushrooms.

Prepare Grilled Mushrooms, *left, omitting the toast and substituting* Garlic Butter, 114, *for the olive oil. Slice and serve as a side dish.*

Grilled New Potatoes with Parsley, Lemon, and Garlic

4 servings

This is basically a grilled version of the classic parsleyed new potatoes, with the smoky taste of the grill adding a new dimension. This recipe also works very well with larger potatoes, but they should be cut into ½-inch slices at the outset.

In a large pot of boiling salted water, cook until easily pierced with a fork but still firm, about 15 minutes:

16 new potatoes, halved

Remove, drain, and allow to cool to room temperature.

Meanwhile, in a small bowl combine and mash together well:

⅓ cup extra virgin olive oil
¼ cup coarsely chopped fresh parsley
2 tablespoons fresh lemon juice
2 teaspoons minced garlic

Salt and ground black pepper to taste

Prepare a medium-hot charcoal fire. Thread the potatoes onto skewers, place on the grill, and cook until well browned, about 7 to 9 minutes per side. Remove from the grill, slide off the skewers into the bowl with the herb-garlic mixture, toss well, and serve.

Grilled Sweet Potatoes with Sweet Chili Glaze

4 to 8 servings

Omit the chili pepper if you want the sweetness without the heat.

Prepare a medium-hot charcoal fire. Cook in a large pot of boiling salted water until easily pierced with a fork but still firm, 5 to 8 minutes:

4 medium sweet potatoes, peeled and cut lengthwise into 1-inch-thick slices

Remove, drain, and allow to cool to room temperature.

Meanwhile, in a medium bowl combine and mash together well:

6 tablespoons light or dark molasses
2 tablespoons light or dark rum
1 tablespoon butter
1 teaspoon minced fresh jalapeño or other chili pepper (optional)
Pinch of ground mace

Salt and ground black pepper to taste

Place the sweet potatoes on the grill rack and grill until browned, 4 to 5 minutes each side. Brush with the molasses mixture, cook for about 30 seconds more each side, remove, and serve.

Autumn Vegetable Hobo Pack

4 servings

You can substitute rutabaga, sweet potatoes, white potatoes, or just about any other root vegetable you wish for those in this recipe. As long as they are all cut into bite-sized pieces, the cooking time should remain about the same. By all means, use other fresh, or even dried, herbs that you like. Take care not to overstuff the packet, or it could be awkward to handle and the vegetables might not cook evenly.

Peel and cut into bite-sized pieces:

2 medium carrots
2 medium beets
2 medium parsnips
1 large red onion
1 medium turnip

Place in large mixing bowl with:

5 cloves garlic, peeled
⅓ cup olive oil
¼ cup coarsely chopped fresh sage, thyme, or oregano
Salt and cracked black peppercorns to taste

Toss lightly and place in the center of a sheet of heavy-duty aluminum foil about 2 feet long. Cover with a second sheet of foil and roll the edges together on all sides, closing the pack. Place in the center of a third length of foil and fold it up around the pack.

Prepare a medium-hot charcoal fire. Place the foil pack in the bottom of the grill and pile coals up on all sides. Cook for 25 to 30 minutes. Remove from the coals, carefully unwrap the foil, and serve at once.

Grilled Bananas

4 servings

Bananas also can be pan-grilled in a ridged cast-iron skillet. Heat the skillet over high heat until very hot but not smoking. Quickly arrange about half the honey-tossed banana pieces crosswise on the ridges. Turn the pieces when they are marked on the bottom and remove them when marked on the second side, about 30 seconds to 1 minute each side. Repeat with the remaining bananas.

Prepare a medium-hot charcoal fire. Peel and cut lengthwise in half:

4 ripe bananas

Cut each half on a diagonal into 3 pieces. Heat in a microwave oven or small saucepan until very fluid:

¼ cup honey

Toss the bananas with the honey in a shallow bowl until all are coated. This can be done 1 to 2 hours in advance.

Arrange the banana pieces crosswise on the grill over hot coals. Grill until marked on the bottom, about 30 seconds to 1 minute each side. Turn and grill just until the second side is marked. Arrange on a platter and dust lightly with:

Ground cinnamon
Ground ginger (optional)

Serve immediately.

Grilled Pineapple with Molasses Glaze

4 servings

This recipe is easily doubled.

Combine in a small saucepan:

2 tablespoons rum
2 tablespoons molasses
2 tablespoons butter
1 tablespoon lime juice

Cook over medium heat, stirring frequently, until the butter is melted and the ingredients are well blended.

Prepare a medium-hot charcoal fire. Rub:

½ ripe pineapple, cut into slices about ½ inch thick

with:

1 tablespoon vegetable oil

Grill for 2 to 4 minutes per side or until the fruit has light grill marks. Turn, brush with the molasses glaze, and grill for 1 minute more. Remove from the grill and serve.

APPROXIMATE GRILLING TIMES FOR FRUIT

Food Type	Fire Temperature	Cooking Time (minutes per side)	Or Until
Apples, *halved*	Medium-low	2 to 3	Golden brown with sear marks
Bananas, *peeled and halved lengthwise*	Medium-low	2 minutes cut side down, 1 minute round side down	Golden brown with sear marks
Pineapple, *½-inch slices*	Medium-low	2 to 4	Slightly seared
Peaches, *pitted and halved*	Medium	5 to 6	Golden brown with sear marks
Plums, *halved*	Medium-low	2 minutes cut side down, 30 seconds skin side down	Slightly seared

Grilled Peaches with Sweet Balsamic Glaze

4 servings

To prevent the peaches from sticking to the grill, oil them very lightly before cooking, but use a light hand. Too much oil not only will interfere with the taste of the fruit but also can cause flare-ups if it drips into the fire.

Combine in a small wide-mouthed saucepan:

1 cup balsamic vinegar

2 tablespoons sugar

1 teaspoon cracked black
**   peppercorns**

Bring to a boil, reduce the heat to low, and simmer, stirring occasionally, for 30 to 45 minutes or until reduced in volume by about two-thirds and thick enough to coat the back of a spoon. Set aside.

Prepare a medium-hot charcoal fire. Lightly brush:

3 firm, ripe peaches, halved and
**   pitted**

with:

1 tablespoon olive oil

Grill the peaches, skin side down, until slightly charred, about 4 to 5 minutes per side. Brush with the glaze and grill until the glaze begins to caramelize slightly, about 1 minute. Remove the peaches from the grill, brush on another layer of glaze, slice into thick slices, and serve, accompanied with:

⅓ cup crumbled blue cheese
**   (optional)**

ABOUT **FLAVOR** ENHANCERS

An easy way to enhance the flavor of meat, poultry, fish, and vegetables is to season them with a savory mixture in the form of a marinade, dry rub, or paste before grilling. The food absorbs the essential oils from the herbs and spices, and when citrus juice, wine, or vinegar is used, the flesh of meat, poultry, fish, or vegetables becomes more tender. Fruity oils, sweetening sugar, and aromatic vegetables also contribute to a more vibrant, more intense taste.

Salsas, chutneys, dipping sauces, relishes, quick pickles, sambals, flavored butters and mayonnaises—even barbecue sauces, spice rubs, and glazes—come under the heading of condiments. They differ widely in what they contain and how they are used, but each occupies the same location in the culinary firmament, somewhere between a single spice and a side dish to be eaten on its own.

The characteristics of condiments tend to shift over time, but they do share a few attributes. All are used to provide flavor for food; all contain more than a single ingredient; all can be made in advance and most can be stored for at least a day or two, often much longer; and all stand alone, created independently and therefore able to add their distinctive flavors to a range of different dishes.

Clockwise from top left: *Tandoori Marinade, 106; West Indies Dry Rub, 108; Fresh Herb Vinaigrette, 110; Green Goddess Dressing, 111; Citrus Herb Marinade, 107*

105

Marinades

A marinade is a seasoned liquid used to flavor food before cooking. Almost all contain some type of acidic ingredient, such as wine, vinegar, or citrus juice, that acts to tenderize the surface of meats, fish, and poultry and to encourage the transfer of flavors. Many marinades, especially those used on vegetables, lean fish, and poultry, often include some olive oil, melted butter, or other fat to baste the food as it cooks. Marinate only in glass, stainless-steel, or food-grade plastic containers, which will not react with the acid. (The glaze on a ceramic bowl may contain toxic lead—you have no way of telling if it does—and acid will draw the lead into the food.) Use a container just large enough to hold the food. Refrigerate food while it marinates, but avoid marinating tender food for too long. Cubed meats marinate for 2 to 3 hours; a whole 5- to 10-pound piece for 12 to 24 hours. Use a stainless-steel or wooden spoon to turn the food and to stir the marinade from time to time. As a general rule, allow 6 to 8 tablespoons of marinade for every 1 pound of food. *Never use the marinade in which raw meat, poultry, or fish has steeped for basting cooked food or as a sauce without first bringing it to a boil to kill any harmful bacteria from the raw food.* Marinades are usually best when prepared fresh. Vinaigrettes also make flavorful marinades. Sprinkling salt over the food before marinating ensures that the food is seasoned evenly. Food to be browned needs to be drained and patted dry; wet food will not brown properly.

Tandoori Marinade

About 1⅓ cups

Whisk together thoroughly:
1 cup yogurt
2 to 3 tablespoons vegetable oil
2 teaspoons finely minced garlic
2 teaspoons finely minced peeled fresh ginger
1 teaspoon ground coriander
1 teaspoon ground cumin
1 teaspoon ground red pepper
1 teaspoon garam masala, or
  ¼ teaspoon ground cinnamon
½ teaspoon ground turmeric
½ teaspoon salt
1 tablespoon yellow food coloring (optional)
1½ teaspoons red food coloring (optional)
Use immediately.

CORIANDER

The flavor of ground coriander is reminiscent of white pepper, cardamom, and cloves with a hint of orange. Ground coriander is made by crushing the small, round ribbed coriander seed.

Citrus Herb Marinade

About ½ cup

This is among the simplest and most satisfying ways to give fish, poultry, meat, and large vegetables lively flavor before applying heat.

Combine in a dish and blend with a fork:

¼ cup mild-tasting olive or nut oil
2½ tablespoons fresh lemon juice
1½ tablespoons fresh orange juice or dry red wine
⅓ cup chopped fresh parsley, preferably flat-leaf
1½ teaspoons dried thyme leaves
½ bay leaf, very finely crumbled
1 clove garlic, minced (optional)
1 teaspoon salt
¼ teaspoon ground black or white pepper, or to taste

Use immediately, or cover and refrigerate for up to 1 week.

> **QUICK CITRUS MARINADE**
> Prepare *Citrus Herb Marinade, left,* omitting the herbs and optional garlic, blending the oil, lemon juice, and orange juice or wine, then seasoning with salt and black or white pepper to taste. Use immediately.

Red Wine Marinade

About 2¼ cups

Excellent for red meats.

Combine in a medium saucepan over low heat and simmer for 2 minutes:

2 cups dry red wine
1 small onion (preferably red), thinly sliced
2 cloves garlic, finely minced
3 sprigs fresh parsley
2 sprigs fresh thyme
6 black peppercorns, cracked
1 small bay leaf
2 whole cloves

Remove from the heat and season with:

Salt to taste

Cover, allow to cool to room temperature, and chill to use as a marinade. This marinade will keep, covered and refrigerated, for up to 1 week.

Balkan Marinade

About 1 cup

This works well with lamb or pork.

Crush together in a nonreactive bowl:

1 tablespoon dried oregano
1 tablespoon dried rosemary
1 teaspoon ground black pepper
1 teaspoon salt

Whisk in:

Juice of 2 lemons
Grated zest of 2 lemons
2 to 4 cloves garlic, minced
¼ cup olive oil
1 teaspoon dried thyme (optional)
3 to 4 drops hot red pepper sauce (optional)
1 tablespoon balsamic vinegar (optional)

Use immediately, or keep, covered and refrigerated, for up to 1 week.

Soy and Sherry Marinade

About 1¼ cups

The combination of soy sauce and dry sherry produces an aromatic and delicious flavor in broiled or grilled chicken and game hen when marinated for only 2 to 3 hours.

Whisk together thoroughly:

½ cup soy sauce
½ cup dry sherry
2 tablespoons Dijon mustard
1 tablespoon hot red pepper sauce
¼ cup vegetable oil

Use immediately, or keep, covered and refrigerated, for up to 1 month.

Dry Rubs, Pastes, Bastes, and Barbecue Sauces

A dry rub is a blend of dried herbs and spices that is rubbed on food before cooking. When a dry rub is moistened with oil or ground fresh ginger or garlic, it becomes a paste.

To use a dry rub or paste, rub the mixture over the entire surface of the food. Naturally, a mild mixture can be applied more thickly than one that is spicy or hot. (Some seasonings produce a handsome finish and some create a tasty crunchy crust, especially in grilling.) Keep any unused rubs and pastes refrigerated for up to a week in tightly covered jars. *Discard any that have come into contact with raw poultry, fish, or meat.*

A baste is a liquid that is brushed onto foods during cooking. It is especially useful when foods are exposed to high temperatures, as in grilling.

A barbecue sauce can be tomato-based or made with a variety of other ingredients. Because it may contain sugar, and can therefore burn, barbecue sauce should be applied only toward the end of grilling; the amount depends on the grill temperature, the sweetness of the sauce, and the size of the food. A nonsweet sauce can be brushed on from start to finish as it is less likely to burn.

Mediterranean Garlic Herb Paste

About 1 ½ cups

Combine in a blender or food processor and coarsely puree, leaving the mixture a little chunky:

10 cloves garlic
1 tablespoon red pepper flakes
2 cups mixed fresh herbs (parsley, sage, rosemary, thyme, basil, and / or oregano)
½ cup olive oil
2 tablespoons salt
¼ cup cracked black peppercorns

Cover and refrigerate until ready to use. This paste will keep, covered and refrigerated, for up to 1 week.

Southern Dry Rub for Barbecue

About 2 cups

Spread in a small dry skillet over medium heat and toast, shaking the pan often to prevent burning, until fragrant, 2 to 3 minutes:

¼ cup cumin seeds

Remove from the heat, let cool to room temperature, and grind to a fine powder in a spice grinder, coffee grinder, or blender, or with a mortar and pestle. Transfer to a small bowl and add:

¼ cup packed brown sugar
½ cup sweet or hot paprika
¼ cup chili powder
2 tablespoons ground red pepper
1 teaspoon ground mace
¼ cup salt
¼ cup cracked black peppercorns

Stir together well. This rub will stay potent, covered and kept in a cool, dark, dry place, for up to 6 weeks.

West Indies Dry Rub

About 1 ¾ cups

Combine in a small dry skillet over medium heat and toast, shaking the pan often to prevent burning, until fragrant, 2 to 3 minutes:

¼ cup cumin seeds
¼ cup coriander seeds

Remove from the heat. Let cool to room temperature, and grind to a fine powder in a spice grinder, coffee grinder, or blender, or with a mortar and pestle. Transfer to a small bowl and add:

¼ cup curry powder
¼ cup ground white pepper
¼ cup ground ginger
¼ cup salt
2 tablespoons ground allspice
2 tablespoons ground red pepper

Stir together well. This rub will stay potent, covered and kept in a cool, dark, dry place, for up to 6 weeks.

Orange-Pineapple-Chipotle Baste

About 3 cups

Combine in a medium saucepan over medium-high heat:

4 cups pineapple juice
2 cups orange juice
2 cups white vinegar
3 tablespoons pureed canned chipotle peppers, or to taste
2 tablespoons ground cumin

Bring to a boil, reduce the heat to medium, and simmer, uncovered, until reduced by about two-thirds, 45 to 60 minutes. Remove from the heat and stir in:

¼ cup fresh lime juice
½ cup chopped fresh cilantro
Salt and cracked black peppercorns to taste

Use hot or at room temperature. This baste will keep, covered and refrigerated, for about 1 month.

Basic Barbecue Sauce

About 2 cups

Apply this sauce during the last 15 minutes of grilling.

Combine in a medium saucepan over medium heat and cook, stirring often, until the sauce comes to a simmer:

1½ cups ketchup
1 cup cider vinegar or red wine vinegar
¼ cup Worcestershire sauce
¼ cup soy sauce
1 cup packed brown sugar
2 tablespoons dry mustard
4 tablespoons chili powder, or to taste
1 tablespoon grated, peeled fresh ginger, or 1 teaspoon ground
2 cloves garlic, minced
2 tablespoons vegetable oil
3 slices lemon

Simmer, stirring often, for 5 minutes. Remove the lemon slices if desired. This sauce will keep, covered and refrigerated, for up to 2 weeks.

Ray's Mustard Barbecue Sauce

About 4 cups

Our friend Chuck Martin's "Uncle Ray" Smith of Lexington County, South Carolina, concocts this classic central South Carolina sauce.

Combine in a medium saucepan and bring to a slow simmer over medium-low heat:

2 cups yellow mustard
½ cup ketchup
½ cup cider vinegar
½ cup vegetable oil
1½ tablespoons ground black pepper
4 cloves garlic, minced
¼ cup onion, grated
⅛ cup Worcestershire sauce
¼ cup honey
Juice of 1 lemon

Simmer five minutes, stirring often to prevent sticking. Remove from heat. The sauce will keep covered, and refrigerated for about 1 month.

Dressings as Marinades or Sauces

A salad dressing is best described as an uncooked sauce and, like all sauces, its role is to enhance the flavor of the food. It should possess a distinct character but never steal the show. A dressing should be well seasoned, typically with a tang of acidity to deliver zest to the food.

Remember that your favorite dressing does not have to be reserved just for salads. Many dressings can be converted into sauces, marinades, or glazes for grilled meat, fish, poultry, or vegetables. When doing so, follow the guidelines given on page 106. The suitability of dressings for such preparations also suggests another popular way to serve grilled foods: atop a bed of crisp greens that have been tossed with your favorite vinaigrette.

Basic Vinaigrette or French Dressing

About 1½ cups

Vinaigrette is the preferred dressing in France for green salads, avocados, artichokes, and many kinds of sliced, shredded, or chopped vegetables. It is also the starting point for a host of more complicated dressings and accepts a variety of accents with additional ingredients. The optional ingredients in this recipe not only add flavor but also help maintain the emulsion of oil and vinegar that is essential to a good vinaigrette.

If garlic flavor is desired, mash together until a paste is formed:

1 small clove garlic, peeled
2 to 3 pinches of salt

Remove to a small bowl or a jar with a tight-fitting lid. Add and whisk or shake until well blended:

⅓ to ½ cup red wine vinegar or fresh lemon juice
1 shallot, minced
1 teaspoon Dijon mustard (optional)
Salt and ground black pepper to taste

Add in a slow, steady stream, whisking constantly, or shake until smooth:

1 cup extra-virgin olive oil

Taste and adjust the seasonings. Use immediately or tightly cover and refrigerate for up to 2 weeks.

FRESH HERB VINAIGRETTE

Use your favorite tender-leafed herb. Prepare *Basic Vinaigrette, left,* adding ⅓ cup minced or finely snipped fresh herbs (basil, dill, parsley, chives, and/or thyme).

LEMON CAPER VINAIGRETTE

Prepare *Basic Vinaigrette, left,* with fresh lemon juice and add 1 tablespoon minced drained capers, 1 tablespoon minced fresh parsley, and ½ teaspoon finely grated lemon zest.

Tangerine Shallot Dressing

About 1½ cups

This dressing is especially good on any salad topped with chicken or even just drizzled over grilled poultry.

Mash together until a paste is formed:

1 clove garlic, peeled
2 to 3 pinches of salt

Remove to a small bowl or a jar with a tight-fitting lid. Add and whisk or shake until well blended:

¼ cup fresh tangerine or clementine juice
2 tablespoons fresh lemon juice
2 small shallots, minced

Add in a slow, steady stream, whisking constantly, or shake until smooth:

⅔ cup vegetable oil

Taste and adjust the seasonings. Use immediately or tightly cover and refrigerate for up to 2 weeks.

Green Goddess Dressing

About 2 cups

This creamy, herby dressing was invented at the historic Palace Hotel in San Francisco in the 1920s in honor of William Archer's hit play The Green Goddess. *It enjoyed great success for decades and is worth a revival.*

Stir together in a small bowl until well blended:

1 cup *Traditional Mayonnaise*, 112, or *Blender Mayonnaise*, 113
½ cup sour cream
¼ cup snipped fresh chives or minced scallions
¼ cup minced fresh parsley
1 tablespoon fresh lemon juice
1 tablespoon white wine vinegar

3 anchovy fillets, rinsed, patted dry, and minced
Salt and ground black pepper to taste

Taste and adjust the seasonings. Use immediately or tightly cover and refrigerate for up to 2 weeks.

Thai Vinaigrette

About ⅔ cup

This vinaigrette, in which the high acidity is balanced by a touch of sweetness, also makes a particularly good marinade for fish or chicken.

Whisk together in a small bowl or shake in a jar with a tight-fitting lid:

¼ cup fresh lime juice
2 tablespoons fish sauce
1 teaspoon sugar
Salt to taste
Ground red pepper to taste

Add in a slow, steady stream, whisking constantly, or shake until smooth:

6 tablespoons vegetable oil

Taste and adjust the seasonings. Use immediately or tightly cover and refrigerate for up to 2 weeks.

Ginger Soy Vinaigrette

About 1 cup

This slightly spicy dressing is particularly nice with watercress salads.

Mash together until a paste is formed:

1 clove garlic, peeled
2 to 3 pinches of salt

Remove to a small food processor or a blender. Add and puree:

¼ cup rice vinegar
¼ cup minced shallots
2 tablespoons minced peeled fresh ginger
1 tablespoon soy sauce
½ teaspoon toasted sesame oil
Salt to taste
Hot red pepper sauce to taste

Slowly pour through the feed tube and process until smooth:

½ cup peanut or vegetable oil

Taste and adjust the seasonings. Use immediately or tightly cover and refrigerate for up to 2 weeks.

Homemade Mayonnaise

If you are accustomed to store-bought mayonnaise, your first taste of homemade will be a surprise. The flavor is bright with lemon juice or vinegar and nutty with good oil. Homemade mayonnaise is elegant and can be made quickly.

Mayonnaise is an emulsion—a stable liquid mixture in which one liquid is suspended in tiny globules throughout another, as with egg yolks in oil (mayonnaise) or in butter (hollandaise). The oil you choose will be the predominant flavor. Made entirely with a robust olive or walnut oil, the sauce will suit equally full-flavored foods—rich meats and aromatic vegetables, for example. For delicate foods, a milder oil is recommended. When mayonnaise is to be the base for other flavors, make it with mild-tasting peanut, safflower, grape-seed, or corn oil. For general use, a balance of fruity and mild oils is most satisfying. Usually three parts mild to one part fruity oil is about right. The oil must be very fresh. One tinge of rancidity and the sauce is all but inedible, so taste the oil before you start. The eggs must also be very fresh; as eggs age, they lose their ability to stabilize an emulsion.

Making the sauce in a food processor or blender or with an electric mixer is practically foolproof, and the sauce has great volume and a fluffy texture. For the finest and silkiest texture of all, make the sauce by hand.

Traditional Mayonnaise

About 1 cup

This is our basic mayonnaise. It can be whisked to a lighter consistency by gradually adding an appropriately flavored stock, vegetable juice, or even spirits. Use a ceramic, glass, or stainless-steel bowl—aluminum or copper will react with the acid and affect the color and flavor of the sauce.

Whisk together in a medium bowl until smooth and light:

2 large egg yolks

1 to 2 tablespoons fresh lemon juice or white wine vinegar
¼ teaspoon salt
Pinch of ground white pepper

Whisk in by drops until the mixture starts to thicken and stiffen:

1 cup vegetable oil, at room temperature

As the sauce begins to thicken—when about one-third of the oil has been added—whisk in the oil more steadily, making sure each addition is thoroughly blended before adding the next. Should the oil stop being absorbed, whisk vigorously before adding more. Stir in:

Up to 1½ teaspoons Dijon mustard (optional)
Salt and ground black pepper to taste

Serve immediately or refrigerate in a tightly covered jar for 1 to 2 days.

Garlic Mayonnaise (Aïoli)

About 1 cup

Whisk together in a medium bowl until smooth and light:

2 large egg yolks
4 to 6 cloves garlic, finely minced
Salt and ground white pepper to taste

Whisk in by drops until the mixture starts to thicken and stiffen:

1 cup olive oil, or part olive and part safflower or peanut oil, at room temperature

As the sauce begins to thicken, whisk in the oil more steadily, making sure each addition is thoroughly blended before adding the next. Gradually whisk in:

1 teaspoon fresh lemon juice
½ teaspoon cold water

Taste and adjust the seasonings. Serve immediately or refrigerate in a tightly covered jar for 1 to 2 days.

Saffron Garlic Mayonnaise (Rouille)

About 1 cup

Stir together in a small bowl, cover, and let stand for 10 minutes:

¾ teaspoon saffron threads
2 tablespoons hot stock or water

Process to fine crumbs:

1 fresh French roll (not sourdough), crust trimmed

Add ¾ cup of the breadcrumbs to the saffron. Mash with a fork to a loose paste, stirring in, if necessary:

Up to 1 tablespoon hot water

Place in a mortar or small bowl:

1 large dried red chili pepper, seeded

Vigorously pound to a powder with a pestle or sturdy wooden spoon. Add and pound until pureed:

3 small cloves garlic, peeled
⅛ teaspoon coarse salt

Stir in:

1 large egg yolk

Stir in the bread paste bit by bit, then work vigorously until smooth. Following the method for adding oil to mayonnaise, opposite, add:

About ¾ cup olive oil, at room temperature

Let the oil fall to one side of the mortar, while you stir it in without stopping. (If the sauce should start to curdle, stir in a little hot stock or water.) When the mixture has absorbed all the oil it can, season with:

Salt to taste

Cover and refrigerate. Use the same day.

Blender Mayonnaise

About 1 cup

Egg white is needed in machine-made mayonnaise. Beat 1 egg well with a fork to blend the yolk and white, let it settle a few seconds, then measure.

Combine in a blender or food processor:

2 tablespoons well-beaten egg
1 large egg yolk
¼ teaspoon dry or Dijon mustard

Process on high speed until well blended, about 5 seconds in a blender, 15 seconds in a food processor fitted with the plastic blade, 30 seconds in a food processor fitted with the steel blade. Scrape down the sides, then sprinkle with:

1 teaspoon fresh lemon juice
¼ teaspoon salt

Process for about 2 minutes in a blender, 15 seconds in a food processor fitted with the plastic blade, 7 to 8 seconds in a food processor fitted with the steel blade. Have ready in a small spouted measuring pitcher:

¾ cup oil, at room temperature

With the machine running, add the oil in the thinnest possible stream. After about one-third of the oil has been added—the mixture will have swollen and stiffened—add the oil in a slightly thicker stream. Stop the machine when all of the oil has been added and scrape down the sides and around the blade, mixing in any unabsorbed oil.

Taste the mayonnaise and stir in:

1½ to 3 teaspoons fresh lemon juice
½ to 1 teaspoon dry or Dijon mustard
Salt and ground white pepper to taste

Serve immediately, or refrigerate in a tightly covered jar for 1 to 2 days.

Flavored Butters (Beurres Composés)

Made by blending herbs or other flavorings into plain butter, these are versatile, quick to make, and easy to store. Flavored butters are served either cold or at room temperature, as decorative garnishes or as instant sauces. They can also be used in place of plain butter for bread or rolls and as an ingredient in complex sauce recipes.

There are two basic types of flavored butters: cooked and uncooked. Cooked ones are browned to various degrees, mixed with other ingredients, and usually served warm as simple sauces for grilled, broiled, sautéed, or steamed foods. Uncooked flavored butters are simply softened butter mixed with spices, herbs, or other pureed or chopped ingredients. The butter can be used immediately while still soft, pressed into molds; or rolled into cylinders in pieces of wax or parchment paper, plastic wrap, or aluminum foil, then refrigerated for 1½ to 2 hours, or frozen, and sliced into thin rounds to garnish dishes just before serving.

Allow about 1 tablespoon per serving. (Flavored butters can be frozen for several weeks, but they should not be refrigerated for more than 24 hours.) For both kinds of flavored butters, start with fresh butter of the highest quality, preferably unsalted so you have more leeway for seasoning to taste.

For guests, we sometimes like to smooth the flavored butter into a small bowl in which it just fits and run a fork over the top in a decorative swirl or crosshatch. The butter is served at room temperature with a butter knife.

Basic Flavored Butter

About ¼ cup

Use this recipe as your formula for preparing any uncooked flavored butter. The variations at right suggest five classic flavoring combinations; feel free to let your imagination and personal tastes guide you in creating others.
In a small bowl, cream with a fork or wooden spoon:

4 tablespoons (½ stick) butter (preferably unsalted), softened
Gradually stir in flavorings as desired along with:

Salt and ground white pepper to taste
Roll the mixture into a cylinder in a piece of wax or parchment paper, plastic wrap, or aluminum foil and refrigerate or freeze until firm enough to slice. Or refrigerate in a small bowl or ramekin and spoon on just before serving.

ANCHOVY BUTTER

For fish, steak, and lamb chops.
Prepare *Basic Flavored Butter, left,* and add 1 teaspoon anchovy paste, ¼ teaspoon fresh lemon juice, or to taste, and salt and ground red pepper to taste.

ORANGE BUTTER

For fish and vegetables.
Prepare *Basic Flavored Butter, left,* and add the finely grated zest of 1 orange, 1 tablespoon strained fresh orange juice, or to taste, a pinch of ground red pepper, and salt to taste.

MAÎTRE D'HÔTEL BUTTER

Traditionally served over steak.
Prepare *Basic Flavored Butter, left,* and add ¾ tablespoon finely chopped parsley and ¾ to 1½ tablespoons fresh lemon juice.

GARLIC BUTTER

For vegetables, steaks, chops, chicken, fish, and shellfish. Blanched garlic has a sweeter, milder flavor than raw garlic.
Prepare *Basic Flavored Butter, left,* and add 1 to 3 cloves garlic, boiled, if desired, in water to cover for 5 to 6 minutes, or left raw, mashed to a paste (with salt if using raw). If desired, add 1 teaspoon minced fresh herbs, such as oregano, marjoram, basil, chervil, or parsley—or a combination.

CRESS OR ARUGULA BUTTER

Wonderfully zippy with root vegetables and other strong flavors.
Prepare *Basic Flavored Butter, left,* and add 1½ teaspoons finely chopped watercress or arugula and a dash of fresh lemon juice.

Mustard Butter

About ⅔ cup

We find this excellent as a rub for small game birds or served on meats and poultry.

Combine in a small bowl:

8 tablespoons (1 stick) unsalted butter, slightly melted

¼ cup Dijon mustard

2 teaspoons honey

1 tablespoon mashed *Roasted Whole Garlic Heads*, right

1 teaspoon minced fresh oregano

2 teaspoons fresh lemon juice

Salt and ground black pepper

Use immediately, or refrigerate in a small bowl or ramekin and spoon on just before serving

---

Roasted Whole Garlic Heads

4 to 6 servings

Choose plump, firm heads of cloves with skins that may be white, purplish, or tinged with red. After roasting, squeeze the garlic pulp from the papery skin.
Preheat the oven to 325°F.
To expose the cloves, cut the top third from:

4 large heads garlic

Place in an 8 × 8-inch baking dish and add:

Enough chicken stock to come one-third up the sides of the heads

Drizzle over the heads:

2 tablespoons olive oil

Place on top of each head:

1 sprig fresh thyme (optional)

Cover with aluminum foil and bake until the garlic is soft and tender, about 1 hour. Serve hot or at room temperature.

Chili Butter

About ⅓ cup

Rub this butter under the skin of poultry or wildfowl before grilling.
Heat in a small skillet over medium heat:

2 tablespoons olive oil

Add and cook, stirring, until softened:

½ cup minced shallots or scallions

4 cloves garlic, finely chopped

Remove to a small bowl and let cool. Stir in:

4 tablespoons (½ stick) unsalted butter, softened

½ teaspoon ground cinnamon

½ teaspoon ground cumin

1½ tablespoons chili powder

2 tablespoons minced fresh cilantro and/or parsley

1 tablespoon fresh lemon juice

Salt and ground black pepper to taste

Use immediately, or refrigerate in a small bowl or ramekin and spoon on just before serving.

Salsas

Salsa translates as "sauce" from both Italian and Spanish, and in these countries "salsa" can apply to everything from creamy white sauce to brown gravy. Still, when we hear the word *salsa*, it is the Latino tomato-and-chili-pepper-based mixes that spring to mind.

Like ketchups, salsas can go over just about everything on the plate. Although some ingredients can be cooked, the sauce itself should be raw, cool, and garden fresh.

In many instances, the raw onions in these recipes are finely chopped, then rinsed under cold water and sometimes sprinkled with citrus juice before combining with the other ingredients. Hand chopping gives superior texture, and rinsing mellows the onion wonderfully, avoiding any biting aftertaste that may overpower the other flavors of the sauce.

Tomatoes can be seeded, but this is not the traditional way to prepare these fresh, unfussy salsas. When removing the blender's lid after grinding condiments containing chili peppers, avert your face—chili fumes are powerful.

For an extra dimension of flavor in a salsa, mix in a splash of light tequila or dark rum. Salsas are best served at room temperature soon after they are made. When serving salsa as an accompaniment to most grilled recipes, allow 2 to 4 tablespoons per serving.

Roasted Tomato–Chipotle Salsa

About 2 cups

Tomatoes take on a deep flavor when roasted. This salsa (opposite, bottom right) is particularly good with grilled chicken and lamb.

Prepare a medium-low charcoal fire. Place on the grill:

6 medium, ripe tomatoes, halved and, if desired, seeded

Grill as close to the heat as possible, carefully turning as needed, until the skins are blackened in spots and slightly softened, about 5 minutes each side. When cool enough to handle, remove the skins and coarsely chop the tomatoes, put them in a medium bowl, and stir in:

1 small onion, finely chopped, rinsed, and drained

¼ cup coarsely chopped fresh cilantro

3 tablespoons fresh lime juice, or to taste

2 tablespoons olive oil

2 cloves garlic, finely chopped

1½ teaspoons finely chopped canned chipotle pepper, or to taste

1 teaspoon ground cumin

Salt to taste

Serve immediately.

Corn, Cherry Tomato, and Avocado Salsa

About 2 cups

Cherry tomatoes are usually the first round tomatoes in season. Their skins are relatively tough, but their flesh is sweet and juicy.

Boil in salted water to cover for 1 minute, drain, and remove the kernels from:

2 ears sweet corn, husked and silk removed

Place the corn kernels in a medium bowl along with:

8 small cherry tomatoes, seeded, if desired, and halved

1 small ripe avocado, peeled and coarsely chopped

¼ cup coarsely chopped fresh basil

½ small red onion, finely diced, rinsed, and drained

2 tablespoons fresh lime juice, or to taste

2 tablespoons vegetable oil

1 clove garlic, finely chopped

1 to 3 fresh jalapeño peppers, seeded and finely chopped

Salt and ground black pepper to taste

Stir together well and serve immediately. This salsa (opposite, upper right) will keep, covered and refrigerated, for 1 day.

Mango Salsa

About 3 cups

Use this salsa (above, left) as a master recipe for fruit salsas—wonderful with just about any food but particularly with grilled fish. Papaya, pineapple, peaches, or apricots can be substituted for the mango; basil or parsley can stand in for the cilantro; and pineapple or guava juice is a good alternative to the orange juice.

Combine in a large bowl:

¼ cup fresh lime juice

1 small red onion, chopped, rinsed, and drained

Prepare the following ingredients, setting them aside, then add all together to the onion mixture:

1 large ripe mango, peeled, pitted, and coarsely chopped

1 small red bell pepper, cut into thin strips

¼ cup coarsely chopped fresh cilantro

1 clove garlic, minced

¼ cup fresh orange juice

1 fresh jalapeño or other small chili pepper, finely chopped

Stir together well. Season with:

Salt and cracked black peppercorns to taste

Serve immediately. This salsa will keep, covered and refrigerated, for 1 day.

Relishes, Chutneys, and Pickles

Nearly every cuisine has created small dishes to be served on the side, designed to enhance the main dishes. Whether called relishes, sambals, chutneys, or garnishes, most are in the realm of condiments, being savory, piquant, spicy, or salty. When selecting one to serve, look for contrast—colors, textures, shapes, and flavors different from the main dish. Most relishes are best cold or at room temperature. Traditional Indian chutneys are fresh; long-cooked chutneys are a British invention. Fresh chutneys are quickly made, brilliantly seasoned, and enormously refreshing.

The deep, complex robust flavors that distinguish ripened cheese from cream are the same that distinguish a dill pickle from a cucumber. Pickles on the table, like sweet preserves, perk up the spirits. In one bite, pickles can mingle our four taste sensations: salty, sour, bitter, and sweet.

Green Tomato Relish

About 6 pints

Combine in a large bowl:

8 pounds green tomatoes, thinly sliced

2¾ pounds onions, thinly sliced

Sprinkle with:

½ cup salt

Stir together well, cover, and refrigerate for 12 hours. Rinse in cold water and drain. Combine in a 4-quart nonreactive saucepan and bring to a boil, stirring until the sugar is dissolved:

1½ quarts cider vinegar

2 pounds brown sugar

Stir in:

2 pounds green bell peppers, sliced

1 pound red bell peppers, diced

6 cloves garlic, minced

1 tablespoon dry mustard

1½ teaspoons salt

Add the tomatoes and onions and stir together well. Tie in a moist square of cloth and add to the saucepan:

1 tablespoon whole cloves

1 tablespoon ground ginger

1½ teaspoons celery seeds

One 3-inch cinnamon stick, broken

Simmer, stirring often, until the tomatoes are translucent, about 1 hour. Let cool, remove the spice bag, then refrigerate in tightly covered pint jars for up to 1 month.

GREEN TOMATOES

Green tomatoes, like green bell peppers, are unripe and come in every size and shape. They may be puckery tart, with crisp flesh not unlike that of a tart green apple. At the end of the season, home gardeners often need to pick tomatoes while still green, making the tomatoes excellent candidates for canning. It should be noted that most tomatoes that are sold commercially are picked at the hard, green, relatively indestructible stage. These tomatoes are then ripened with gas (no sun in sight).

Red Onion Marmalade

About 2 cups

Onion marmalade is wonderful with grilled meats.

Combine in a medium nonreactive saucepan over low heat:

3½ large red onions, cut into ¼-inch-thick slices, halved crosswise

⅓ cup dry red wine

⅓ cup red wine vinegar

¼ cup packed light brown sugar

¼ cup mild honey

Cook, stirring, until the sugar is dissolved; then simmer, stirring often, until the consistency of marmalade, about 30 minutes. Stir in:

1 tablespoon orange juice

1 tablespoon lemon juice

Continue to cook, stirring, until the juices are absorbed. Let cool, then cover and refrigerate for up to 3 weeks. Serve at room temperature.

Tart Corn Relish

About 10 pints

Blanch for 5 minutes in boiling salted water (1 teaspoon salt to every 1 quart water):

18 medium ears yellow or bicolor corn, husked and silk removed

Dip in cold water, then pat dry. Cut off the kernels, without scraping, into a very large container. Add:

1 pound red bell peppers, chopped

8 ounces green bell peppers, chopped

4 ounces mild green chili peppers, seeded and chopped

1½ pounds red onions, chopped

12 ounces green or red cabbage, chopped

5 cups cider vinegar

1 cup sugar

1 cup water

½ cup fresh lemon juice

3 tablespoons chopped fresh dill, or 1½ teaspoons dried dill

2 tablespoons salt

2 teaspoons yellow mustard seeds

2 teaspoons ground turmeric

1 teaspoon celery seeds

Mix until well blended. Whisk until smooth in a small bowl:

1 cup water

½ cup all-purpose flour

Cook the vegetables in 2 batches in a large nonreactive saucepan. Bring half of the vegetables to a boil over high heat, then reduce the heat and simmer, stirring often, for 10 minutes. Stir in half the reserved flour mixture, and cook, stirring occasionally until it thickens, then more often, for 10 minutes more. Repeat with the remaining vegetables and flour mixture. Let cool. Cover and refrigerate in jars for up to 1 month.

Quick Red Onion Pickle

About 2 cups

Red onions are usually on the sweet side. Some red onions are red only down through the first layer; when you find a market that stocks onions that are red through and through, stick with it. When selecting onions, choose those that are tightly closed and very firm. This quick pickle is a perfect accompaniment to grilled chicken or steak.

Combine in a medium bowl:

⅓ cup red wine vinegar

2 tablespoons sugar

1 tablespoon grenadine (optional)

1 tablespoon cracked black peppercorns

Add and let marinate for 2 hours:

2 red onions, cut into ¼-inch-thick slices and separated into rings

Serve immediately. This pickle will keep, covered and refrigerated, for up to 2 days.

Fresh Mint Chutney

About ⅔ cup

Delicious with vegetables, fish and poultry. In India, mint chutney is prized for its digestive properties, and accompanies fried and highly spiced dishes.

Combine in a food processor or blender and process to a coarse puree, stopping to scrape down the sides as needed:

1 cup fresh peppermint or other mint leaves

¼ large onion, cut into 1-inch pieces

5 tablespoons cold water

2 tablespoons fresh lime or lemon juice

2 teaspoons sugar

¼ teaspoon coarse salt

⅛ teaspoon ground red pepper, or to taste

Cover and refrigerate for no longer than 1 day. Serve in a small bowl.

Fresh Pineapple Chutney

About 2½ cups

Peel and quarter lengthwise:

1 ripe sweet pineapple (about 2½ pounds)

Core each quarter and discard, cut the pineapple into bite-sized chunks, then cut each chunk in half with the grain. Combine in a medium nonreactive saucepan with:

2 fresh red or green serrano peppers, seeded and minced

2 tablespoons sugar

¼ teaspoon ground cinnamon

¼ teaspoon salt

Pinch of ground cloves

Bring to a boil, then simmer, stirring often. Continue to simmer, stirring often, until the pineapple is just tender, 15 to 20 minutes. Serve hot or at room temperature, or keep, covered and refrigerated, for 12 hours.

Ketchups

We got our ketchup from the British in the nineteenth century, and they got theirs from the Far East long before. The word is derived from the Malay word *kechap*, a fish sauce. No other food so familiar seems to have so many spellings. In England, it is both pronounced and written "ketchup," while both "catsup" and "ketchup" are used in the United States. In the beginning, ketchups resembled today's unsweetened Asian seasoning sauces—thin, sharp, and dark. Some were concocted from tomato juice, but many were based on mushrooms, walnuts, anchovies, or oysters. Sugar was not added until the end of the nineteenth century, and in today's commercial ketchups, sweetening is the second ingredient—after tomato concentrate and before the garlic and onion powders. The ketchups we like best are a balance of tangy and sweet.

Blender Tomato Ketchup

About 9 pints

Both the flavoring and the cooking make this an old-fashioned ketchup without the old-fashioned work (opposite, right). Halving the amounts is not recommended, as simmering in smaller batches detrimentally affects flavor, texture, and the critical acid content. Instead, divide up your finished batch to share with family and friends.

In manageable batches, process in a blender until pureed, about 5 seconds each batch:

24 pounds ripe tomatoes, peeled and quartered

2 pounds onions, quartered
1 pound red bell peppers, cut into strips
1 pound green bell peppers, cut into strips

Remove to a large nonreactive pot. Stir together well and bring to a boil, stirring often, over medium heat. Simmer, stirring often and thoroughly, for 1 hour. Stir in:

9 cups cider vinegar
9 cups sugar
¼ cup canning or pickling salt

Tie in a moist square of cloth and add to the tomato mixture:

3 tablespoons dry mustard
1½ tablespoons sweet or hot paprika
1½ tablespoons whole allspice
1½ tablespoons whole cloves
Two 3-inch cinnamon sticks

Continue simmering and stirring until the mixture is reduced by half and mounds up on a spoon with no separation of liquid and solids. Remove and discard the spice bag. Let cool, then cover and refrigerate for up to 1 month.

Red Onion–Garlic Ketchup

About 3 cups

This ketchup (opposite, left) is perfect with grilled steak or hamburgers.

Heat in a large nonreactive skillet over medium heat:

⅓ cup olive oil

Add and cook, stirring often, until well browned, about 10 to 20 minutes:

5 large red onions, thinly sliced

Stir in and cook until the garlic and ginger are softened, about 3 minutes:

¼ cup minced garlic
1 tablespoon minced peeled fresh ginger
1 medium, ripe tomato, finely diced

Add:

1 teaspoon hot red pepper sauce, or to taste
5 tablespoons Worcestershire sauce
½ cup light or dark molasses
¾ cup cider vinegar
1 teaspoon ground allspice

Reduce the heat to low and cook, stirring occasionally, until slightly thickened, about 15 minutes. Remove from the heat and season with:

Salt and ground black pepper to taste

Let cool to room temperature. Once the mixture has cooled, place it in a blender or food processor and puree. Serve warm or cold. This will keep, covered and refrigerated, for up to 1 month.

An International Sampler of Cold Sauces

All around the world, creative cooks have come up with cold sauces combining favorite regional flavors that perfectly complement the taste of foods from the grill. The beauty of the sauces on these pages is how easily yet dramatically they can transform a simple grilled dish. Consider, for example, the different dining experiences that can result from accompanying a steak with the rich bite of *American Horseradish Cream, below,* the lively herbaceous character of Argentine *Chimichurri, below,* or the sweet-sour tang of Cuban *Mojo, opposite.* All these sauces are easily made in advance and may be refrigerated for 2 to 3 days.

American Horseradish Cream

About 1 ¼ cups

An unexpected combination, a particular delight with simply grilled beef, hot or cold. Prepared horseradish can be found in the grocery deli case.
Beat until stiff:
½ cup chilled heavy cream

Gradually add, beating constantly:
3 tablespoons fresh lemon juice or cider vinegar
2 tablespoons grated horseradish or drained prepared white horseradish

¼ teaspoon salt
Pinch of ground red pepper
Chill for 30 minutes to 1 hour, then serve.

Scandinavian Mustard-Dill Sauce

About 1 cup

This sauce is perfect with grilled fish.
Whisk together in a medium bowl until smooth:
3 tablespoons Swedish or Dijon mustard
2 tablespoons snipped fresh dill
1 to 2 tablespoons sugar

2 tablespoons fresh lemon juice or red wine vinegar, or to taste
Salt and ground black pepper to taste
Pinch of ground cardamom
Gradually add, whisking constantly, until blended and smooth:

½ cup vegetable oil
Cover and let stand for 2 to 3 hours before serving to allow the flavors to develop. Serve at room temperature or chilled. This sauce will keep, covered and refrigerated, for up to 2 days.

Chimichurri

About 1 ¼ cups

The Argentineans are enthusiastic meat eaters and often serve grilled or roasted meat with this slightly spicy sauce (opposite, right) on the side. Some Argentine cooks prefer the less distinctive flavor of corn oil to the olive oil used here, and may substitute half the quantity of dried oregano for the fresh herb.
Whisk together thoroughly in a small bowl:

½ cup olive oil
¼ cup red wine vinegar
Stir in:
1 small onion, finely chopped
⅓ cup finely chopped fresh parsley or cilantro
4 cloves garlic, finely chopped
1 tablespoon finely chopped fresh oregano (optional)
Salt to taste

¼ teaspoon ground red pepper, or to taste
¼ teaspoon ground black pepper, or to taste
Cover and let stand for 2 to 3 hours before serving to allow the flavors to develop. This sauce will keep, covered and refrigerated, for up to 2 days.

Mojo

About 1 cup

The national table sauce of Cuba, mojo (above, left) is a colorful version of the familiar vinaigrette. Traditionally made with the fresh juice of the sour orange, it can also be made with fresh lime juice and, for variation, grapefruit or pineapple juice. Feel free to experiment with your own blend of two or more juices. Unlike most vinaigrettes, mojo is briefly cooked to bring out the full flavor of the garlic. Use caution when adding the juice to the hot oil, as it may splatter. A deep saucepan is a wise precaution. Mojo can be stored for a few days, but it is best when served fresh. This condiment for grilled meat, poultry, or seafood goes especially well with pork. If you like, try using it as a marinade or baste, following the guidelines given on 106–109.

Heat in a medium saucepan over medium heat:

½ cup olive oil

Add and cook until fragrant but not browned, 20 to 30 seconds:

8 cloves garlic, minced

Remove from the heat and let cool for 5 minutes. Carefully stir in and bring to a boil:

**¾ cup fresh lime, grapefruit, or
   pineapple juice**

¾ teaspoon ground cumin

**Salt and ground black pepper
   to taste**

Let cool and serve at room temperature. This sauce will keep, covered and refrigerated, for up to 3 days.

Tapenade (Caper Olive Paste)

About 2¾ cups

The one ingredient required by tradition in this popular spread is the caper—tapeno in Provençal. Tapenade (above, upper right) made without capers or with only a hint of them is sometimes called olivade.

Combine in a food processor and pulse until the mixture is coarse but of a uniform consistency:

2 cups black olives, preferably oil cured, pitted
3 anchovies, rinsed and patted dry (optional)
3 tablespoons drained capers
2 tablespoons brandy or fresh lemon juice
3 tablespoons extra-virgin olive oil
2 cloves garlic, coarsely chopped
2 teaspoons fresh thyme leaves, or 1 teaspoon dried
Salt and ground black pepper to taste

Serve with:

Crusty French bread

Harissa

About ⅓ cup

In North Africa, this fiery pepper paste (opposite, far left) is stirred into black olives, seafood stews, soups, herb salads, and vegetable dishes, or used as an ingredient in sauces for brochettes, tagines, and couscous.

Combine in a small dry skillet over medium heat and toast, shaking the pan often to prevent burning, until very aromatic, 2 to 3 minutes:

1 teaspoon caraway seeds
1 teaspoon coriander seeds
½ teaspoon cumin seeds

Remove from the heat, let cool to room temperature, and grind to a fine powder in a spice grinder, coffee grinder, or blender, or with a mortar and pestle. Add and grind again until smooth:

2 cloves garlic, quartered
Salt to taste

Add and grind until all ingredients are well combined:

3 tablespoons sweet paprika
1 tablespoon red pepper flakes
1 tablespoon olive oil

The harissa will be very thick and dry. Transfer the paste to a small jar and cover with:

Olive oil

Store, covered, in the refrigerator; it will keep for 6 months.

Citrus Sauce

About ½ cup

A perfect sauce for grilled foods, especially fish.

With a sharp knife, remove the peel and all the white pith from:

2 navel oranges
1 small lemon

Holding the fruit over a bowl to catch the juices, use a knife to free the orange and lemon sections with as little membrane as possible; let the sections fall into the bowl. Squeeze out the remaining juice after removing all the sections. Stir in:

¼ cup extra-virgin olive oil
**Salt and ground white pepper
    to taste**

Serve at room temperature, or cover and refrigerate for up to 1 day.

Fresh Tomato Sauce

About 3 cups

Summer's best. Make this easy sauce when you can get juicy, ripe tomatoes.

Drain in a colander for 20 minutes:

**5 large ripe tomatoes, seeded and
    finely diced**

Remove to a large bowl and stir in:

**½ cup fresh basil leaves, finely
    chopped**
3 tablespoons extra-virgin olive oil
2 cloves garlic, finely minced
**Salt and ground black pepper
    to taste**

Let stand for at least 30 minutes. Serve the sauce at room temperature. If serving over hot pasta, sprinkle each portion with:

1 to 2 teaspoons balsamic vinegar

Salsa Verde

About 1 cup

Serve this classic Italian sauce (opposite, bottom right) with grilled fish.

Place in a food processor and blend to uniform consistency, but do not overprocess:

⅔ cup parsley leaves
2½ tablespoons drained capers
6 anchovy fillets (optional)
**½ teaspoon red wine vinegar, or
    1 tablespoon freshly squeezed
    lemon juice**
½ teaspoon finely chopped garlic
½ teaspoon strong mustard
½ cup extra-virgin olive oil
Salt to taste

Adjust seasonings. Serve at room temperature or store, covered and refrigerated, up to 1 week.

Index

Bold type indicates that a recipe has an accompanying photograph.

ACKNOWLEDGMENTS

Special thanks to my wife and editor in residence, Susan; our indispensable assistant and comrade, Mary Gilbert; and our friends and agents, Gene Winick and Sam Pinkus. Much appreciation also goes to Simon & Schuster, Scribner, and Weldon Owen for their devotion to this project. Thank you Carolyn, Susan, Bill, Marah, John, Terry, Roger, Gaye, Val, Norman, and all the other capable and talented folks who gave a part of themselves to the Joy of Cooking All About series.

My eternal appreciation goes to the food experts, writers, and editors whose contributions and collaborations are at the heart of Joy—especially Stephen Schmidt. He was to the 1997 edition what Chef Pierre Adrian was to Mom's final editions of Joy. Thank you one and all.

Ethan Becker

FOOD EXPERTS, WRITERS, AND EDITORS

Selma Abrams, Jody Adams, Samia Ahad, Bruce Aidells, Katherine Alford, Deirdre Allen, Pam Anderson, Elizabeth Andoh, Phillip Andres, Alice Arndt, John Ash, Nancy Baggett, Rick and Deann Bayless, Lee E. Benning, Rose Levy Beranbaum, Brigit Legere Binns, Jack Bishop, Carole Bloom, Arthur Boehm, Ed Brown, JeanMarie Brownson, Larry Catanzaro, Val Cipollone, Polly Clingerman, Elaine Corn, Bruce Cost, Amy Cotler, Brian Crawley, Gail Damerow, Linda Dann, Deirdre Davis, Jane Spencer Davis, Erica De Mane, Susan Derecskey, Abigail Johnson Dodge, Jim Dodge, Aurora Esther, Michele Fagerroos, Eva Forson, Margaret Fox, Betty Fussell, Mary Gilbert, Darra Goldstein, Elaine Gonzalez, Dorie Greenspan, Maria Guarnaschelli, Helen Gustafson, Pat Haley, Gordon Hamersley, Melissa Hamilton, Jessica Harris, Hallie Harron, Nao Hauser, William Hay, Larry Hayden, Kate Hays, Marcella Hazan, Tim Healea, Janie Hibler, Lee Hofstetter, Paula Hogan, Rosemary Howe, Mike Hughes, Jennifer Humphries, Dana Jacobi, Stephen Johnson, Lynne Rossetto Kasper, Denis Kelly, Fran Kennedy, Johanne Killeen and George Germon, Shirley King, Maya Klein, Diane M. Kochilas, Phyllis Kohn, Aglaia Kremezi, Mildred Kroll, Loni Kuhn, Corby Kummer, Virginia Lawrence, Jill Leigh, Karen Levin, Lori Longbotham, Susan Hermann Loomis, Emily Luchetti, Stephanie Lyness, Karen MacNeil, Deborah Madison, Linda Marino, Kathleen McAndrews, Alice Medrich, Anne Mendelson, Lisa Montenegro, Cindy Mushet, Marion Nestle, Toby Oksman, Joyce O'Neill, Suzen O'Rourke, Russ Parsons, Holly Pearson, James Peterson, Marina Petrakos, Mary Placek, Maricel Presilla, Marion K. Pruitt, Adam Rapoport, Mardee Haidin Regan, Peter Reinhart, Sarah Anne Reynolds, Madge Rosenberg, Nicole Routhier, Jon Rowley, Nancy Ross Ryan, Chris Schlesinger, Stephen Schmidt, Lisa Schumacher, Marie Simmons, Nina Simonds, A. Cort Sinnes, Sue Spitler, Marah Stets, Molly Stevens, Christopher Stoye, Susan Stuck, Sylvia Thompson, Jean and Pierre Troisgros, Jill Van Cleave, Patricia Wells, Laurie Wenk, Caroline Wheaton, Jasper White, Jonathan White, Marilyn Wilkenson, Carla Williams, Virginia Willis, John Willoughby, Deborah Winson, Lisa Yockelson.

Weldon Owen wishes to thank the following people for their generous assistance and support in producing this book: Desne Border, Ina Chow, Ken DellaPenta, and Joan Olson.